THE PLAY PRODUCED

SOME PRESS OPINIONS.

THE PLAY PRODUCED

An Introduction to the Technique
of Producing Plays

BY

JOHN FERNALD

FOREWORD BY

FLORA ROBSON

Price................*80*.....*P*.Net

KENYON - DEANE LTD.
LONDON

Printed in Great Britain by
Latimer Trend & Co Ltd, Whitstable
Reprinted in Belgium by Jos Adam, Brussels

FOREWORD

I ESTEEM it a great privilege to write the foreword to Mr. Fernald's excellent book.

You will find, as I did, in reading this book, that it makes explicit many points of technique which you may have known by experience or instinct, but which you have not been able to formulate clearly. This is exactly what the producer requires, for he must have a definite and thorough knowledge of every branch of the theatre.

In every art, you must know all the rules existing before you can break them with impunity. This book, without being dogmatic, gives you most of the important rules of our day. It is the producer's business to know the " works," but he should never let the audience " see the wheels going round." Mr. Fernald very clearly shows us the " works " of a play, and its production. His analogies and similes are particularly helpful.

A play must make an instantaneous appeal. It is not like a book, where, when you have forgotten some detail, you can easily refer back to an earlier chapter ; each point must be made clear to prevent the audience's impressions becoming blurred. Mr. Fernald rightly insists on clarity and simplicity in a production. A good production looks so easy and the acting so spontaneous, that I have known quite intelligent people to be surprised that you have to rehearse a play, or that you require a producer. Indeed, the fact that there *is* a technique in making the audience laugh or cry is something in the nature of a fraud to them.

An actor may have all the emotion in the world and never make people cry, and a great sense of humour and never make them laugh, and so technique, the building of a scene, becomes all important.

The chapter on Form in production is of great interest, and an answer to those who think that actors can " produce " themselves.

An actor is helped in the portrayal of a character as much by the behaviour of the other players round him, as by his own performance. To take a very simple instance ; in playing the part of a King, you will not have much chance to convey your dignity if your gentlemen show you no respect and talk among themselves. Every part is interdependent, and there must be one conception only of each part, to make interplay possible.

Mr. Fernald shows a great respect for the actor. His principle " to see that the actor agrees with him about any particular effect that is desired, but to leave to the actor's own judgment the method of obtaining that effect " is one that would win the confidence of any actor, but very rightly Mr. Fernald adds, " Most actors have an inherent and understandable tendency to overestimate the importance of their individual parts." We all know the man who has one line to say, and asks every member of the company, " Should I say, ' the CARRIAGE is here ' or ' the carriage IS here ' or ' the carriage is HERE ' ? " But the star who wants attention focussed upon himself the whole time is just as deplorable.

The comparison of the producer to an orchestral conductor is particularly apt. I wonder what would happen in the performance of a symphony, if a trumpeter suddenly thought, " This is a nice bit, I will play it louder ! ! "

The whole theory of balance in a production, and of the focal point or position of dramatic dominance is made completely clear. Mr. Fernald shows the importance of other actors " fading out " when it is necessary that the audience should concentrate on one particular point. But his advice to the actor to continue silently to act " so that, when his turn comes, he will be able to slip smoothly into the emotional key which the other characters have given to the scene," seems to me exactly what is wanted.

As a text-book to producers, this small volume has every branch explained with great clarity, but no less is it of value to actors in helping to convey the producer's aim of a completely unified scheme.

FLORA ROBSON.

CONTENTS

THE PLAY PRODUCED

I. INTRODUCTION

IT is a misfortune of the stage producer that while in professional quarters he is taken for granted, the general public refuses to believe that he even exists. Yet there is not a single play performed—be it professional or amateur—which has not had a producer of some sort ; so that a book which attempts to explain something of his methods may be of interest to those whose enthusiasm for the theatre is greater than their knowledge of its technique.

To the amateur stage in particular it is hoped that it may be of some service, for here the need of some sort of instruction in producing plays is often great indeed. Too frequently amateur societies are forced, in the absence of a suitable producer, to employ the local teacher of elocution, whose knowledge of the human glottis does not compensate for the fact that she is often ignorant of the art of stage production.

Such a state of affairs cannot be blamed on the amateur, for he has always taken his lead from the professional stage. And the professional stage has created scores of dramatic schools, which have turned out scores of actors and actresses, who have in turn written countless books on the *art of acting*, some of which are invaluable to the amateur in learning his job. But there is no professional school of *producing* :

the professional producer has to learn by his own mistakes. Moreover, he is a comparatively rare bird, and his influence upon the amateur theatre is correspondingly slight. Hence—the amateur theatre, while it is steadily attaining a high level of acting ability, is not getting the instruction it needs in how that ability should be used.

It should be no part of the producer's duty to teach people how to act, although with amateurs it frequently falls to his lot to have to do so : the elocution teachers and the dramatic schools are competent enough for this purpose. Actors are part of the producer's material : he expects them to be efficient, just as an artist demands purity in his pigments, and he has to employ their qualities to the best advantage for the proper expression of the play to be presented. He is (as Mr. Ashley Dukes points out in his admirable book " Drama "[1]) analogous to the orchestral conductor, and his actors are a company of soloists whose performances he has to mould into a proper *ensemble*. Although, unfortunately sometimes, he cannot control his players during the actual performance of the play, he has yet to " conduct " that performance during the period of rehearsals : he is responsible for the actors' movements, for their positions upon the stage, for the manner and *tempo* of their speech, as well as for the scenery, lighting, effects and every other detail of the complete production.

Undoubtedly the producer must be something of a Pooh-Bah of the theatre. In his constitution there must be something of the actor, something of the musician, something of the pictorial artist—and something of generalship. But these qualities must be exercised with the greatest subtlety and restraint.

[1] Home University Library, Williams and Norgate, 2s.

He must not act the actor's part for him ; he must not overburden the play with " trick " production and over-elaborate settings : above all, his influence on a performance, though firm and definite, must pass almost unnoticed by the audience, and as often as not, by the actor himself.

It is for this latter reason, perhaps, that the majority of people know so little about his work, and that in some quarters it has even been said to be unnecessary. We are often told that the producer is a comparatively modern invention, that in the great days of Irving and Tree he did not exist, that his influence acts as a stranglehold upon the actor, and that his abolition would do much to bring the theatre back to its former " virility." A little research will soon prove the falsity of these arguments. The Greeks employed a sort of stage manager who controlled to a considerable extent the open-air performances of the Greek theatre ; the various bands of comedians grouped under the label of La Commedia dell' Arte (popularly regarded as the perfect examples of " natural " and " spontaneous " actors) possessed an official called a " Capocomico " who actually produced and directed their rehearsals ; there were producers in the Elizabethan theatre, while in recent times no one was a greater martinet as a producer than Sir Henry Beerbohm Tree himself.

If we look for those dramatic companies which attained the highest collective standard of performance and which excelled for their *team work*, we find in most cases that not only did they employ a producer, but that their producer *was not one of the actors*, or else confined himself to playing parts of minor importance. Particularly was this true of the best companies of the Commedia dell' Arte. In the late Victorian and

Edwardian theatre the importance of this was only too well demonstrated. We hear a great deal of the greatness of Tree and Irving, but not so much of the brilliance of the actors who supported them. For the actor-manager-producer of that period was, from all accounts, far too occupied with his own performance to care very much about those of his cast. If he took trouble with his company it was to make quite certain that none of them should ever become effective enough to steal his own limelight. Tree was indeed a magnificent producer—of his own acting. It is said that in one of his productions he kept the attention of the audience upon him for no less than ten minutes before he was due to speak the first lines of his part—simply by pieces of stage " business " so excellent that no one could take their eyes off him. That some unfortunate actor was at the same time attempting to give a performance and to plant the plot of the play did not matter, for it was Tree's performance that everyone came to see, and the play was a bad one ; plays of that period frequently were.

The audiences of to-day expect a good play as well as good acting ; they expect the play's balance to be preserved ; they demand team work in its performance. And not many actors have that natural sense of team work which might make a producer unnecessary. Most actors have an inherent and understandable tendency to overestimate the importance of their individual parts : for them some form of control is essential if all the dramatic possibilities of the play are to be properly exploited. On the amateur stage this control is even more important, since the natural inventiveness and feeling for the stage of the average amateur is comparatively undeveloped.

To the argument that the proper person to exercise

this control is the author himself, it may be answered that the author, even when he is competent, is seldom available for the purpose. Moreover, the fact that an author can write a good play does not mean that he can express it in terms of the theatre, for the manipulation of acting, movement, *décor*, etc., is a technique often unknown to him. Neither is he often able to take a detached view of his own work ; and the producer's greatest asset is precisely this very quality of detachment, which makes him able to view the play and its performers with a fresh perception, *from the point of view of the audience*. If that producer is also acting he can never do this, for the actor tends to think solely of his part and of his relation to it, while the producer must think of *all* the parts in relation to the play. More than that, he must make himself a sort of advance post for the general public ; he must be able to put himself in the audience's place, and to some extent anticipate its reactions. To this end he acquires a mental attitude and a technique which is all his own.

It must be remembered, however, that in this art, as in any other, mere technique is not enough. He who wishes to become a good producer must *feel* that his capacity is for this branch of the theatre and for no other. He must have a sense of rhythm, and a sense of something akin to music ; he must have a feeling for the meaning and the beauty of words, as well as a sense of composition and of pictorial values. Above all, despite the power that his position as producer gives him, he must be able to use that power with discrimination and restraint. He must not bully his actors. He must not *impose* his rendering of the parts upon them, but must draw from them, almost without their knowing it, the very best that is in them. He must *control*, but he must not *command*. And, perhaps more than anything else, he must remember that his duty is towards the play and its author, and not towards the glorification of himself.

What his technique is, this book will attempt to explain. It will not dwell in any great detail upon the pictorial side of the producer's work, although this is a most important factor in the theatre, and its place in relation to the producer will, it is hoped, be made clear. But it is a factor which has been exhaustively examined elsewhere, and we propose, therefore, to deal mainly with the methods and purpose of the producer in his use of the *actor*. For this, after all, forms the bulk of the work of putting a play on to the stage.

II. THE PRODUCER AND PLAYWRIGHT

" THE Producer is analogous to the orchestral conductor." The difference between a badly produced play and a well-produced play is the difference between a symphony unimaginatively played (though with all its notes correct) by the conductor of some inferior orchestral society, and the same symphony expressed by a distinguished musician at the Queen's Hall. In the first case the words or the notes have been painstakingly and perfectly accurately translated into terms of sound : in the second the full dramatic or musical potentialities of the work have been fully exploited by an imaginative interpreter. Popular criticism of the bad conductor would say that " he brings nothing to it " ; and that, applied to the bad stage producer, would exactly hit the nail on the head.

It is not enough for him simply to transfer the printed play to the stage of a theatre ; to follow faithfully the author's stage directions, and to cause his actors and actresses correctly to learn and speak their parts : *he must bring something to it*. And to do that he must have, not an author's vision of the play, nor an actor's vision of it, nor yet a reader's vision of it—but a producer's vision ; which simply means that he must regard the play, not as a written work, but as a potential *performance*. He must regard it as performed by definite actors with definite individualities, grouping and re-grouping themselves in definite patterns in front of a definite background.

7

The written play then becomes one factor among a number of other factors, such as acting, movement, grouping, *décor*—all of which contribute their quota towards the making of the performance—the piece of " *Theatre*," we shall call it, which is the producer's creation. That the written play is the most important of these factors is obvious enough, for upon its characteristics will depend the characteristics of all the others : the performance—*Theatre*—owes its existence and its individuality to the play—*Drama*. Our first business therefore in our attempt to explain the producer's art is to find out what are those factors in *Drama* to which, in performance, he seeks to give practical expression.

The word " Drama "—comprising as it does the entire range of tragedy, comedy, and farce—is derived from the Greek " δραω," *I do*, and therefore *drama* in its primary sense means the expression of action. Action implies the making of an effort, and effort implies some sort of resistance ; to lift a weight means **Conflict** the conquest of gravity, to move a finger the conquest of inertia. But action, as a basis of the plot of a play, can only become interesting if the resistance against it is considerable—in fact, if it provides some sort of *conflict*. Without conflict there can be no excitement : an audience will soon lose interest in a boxing match where one opponent allows himself to be beaten without putting up a fight. Conflict would seem to be an essential germ of most drama : the plays of Euripides, the tragedies of Shakespeare, the modern " problem play " and the entire realm of Melodrama—these are cases in point. Yet for comedy and farce mere conflict does not seem to provide a true basis. Does the drama cease in a Shakespeare play when the protagonists have left the stage and the audience is enjoying the comic relief of the clowns and fools ? Does "conflict" explain why we laugh at "The Importance of Being Earnest" when John Worthing suddenly appears among a gay assembly sombred in black from top to toe, in mourning for someone who does not exist ?

This is not conflict so much as *contrast*. And contrast would seem to be a basis of comedy : for example, let us imagine two men making a simultaneous entrance upon a stage ; if they are merely two normal men entering together no one will even smile at them ; but if one of them is very long and the other very short a burst of laughter is almost inevitable. The contrast here is of appearance : but it may also be verbal, or of situation, or of character ; and in one form or another, it is a factor common to all comedy.

Now, if we examine the nature of the serious drama with its basis of conflict, we shall find that this conflict, too, is in reality nothing but contrast. For, unlike a boxing match, stage conflict is most dramatic, not through the conflict of evenly matched *similar* forces, but through the conflict of evenly matched *contrasting* forces. A stage fight in which both antagonists suffer and triumph equally and therefore win and lose simultaneously may be laughed at, because of its contrast with reasonable probability, but it cannot be taken seriously. Yet a fight in which *intelligence* is pitted against *brute force* provides an immediate contrast, and cannot fail to be exciting. Here the contrast exists in the characterization of the opponents ; and it is of the characterization of all drama that this quality of *Dramatic Contrast* is an essential basis. The great tragedies manifest them-

Dramatic Contrast

selves in the conflicts of their protagonists, but their true essence lies in the dramatic contrasts between their characters. The tragedy of King Lear consists not so much in the conflict between him and his daughters, as in the result of the dramatic contrast between their young virility and his aged infirmity, and between his downfall and his former glory.

In every play instances of dramatic contrast abound : in plot, in situation, and in characterization. It is, indeed, the very life-blood of drama : it is also the very life-blood of good theatre. But dramatic contrast in the theatre does not merely mean the expression in performance of the dramatic contrast of the written play. This must, it is true, be made apparent ; but the producer must do more than that, since the written play is but one of the factors of which a piece of Theatre is composed. *Through each of the other constituent factors dramatic contrast must be shown ; through the acting, the movement, the grouping and the* décor. Just as a play without contrasts is *undramatic*, a perform- ance without contrasts is *untheatrical*.

A large part of the producer's work now becomes clear. The contrasts—expressed through dialogue— which the author has already created are like the notes and harmonies which the composer bequeaths to the conductor : there is no excuse for misinterpreting them, and in performance it is taken for granted that these, at least, should be right. Similarly it is as a matter of course expected of a producer that he should give proper expression to what the playwright has pre- sented to him. But his work " of bringing something " to the play begins with *the supplementing of the author's contrasts with a perpetual variety in the performance.*

Another part of his work consists in the actual inter- pretation of the author's dialogue. The significance of the words of a play depends, not only upon their context, but upon the tone, volume and pace at which they are said. Dialogue may mean that which upon the surface it appears to mean ; but the tone in which it is spoken may imply the very reverse. The author characterizes his people by the words he gives them : the producer supplements this characterization by determining *how* those words shall be spoken, through a manipulation of the various dramatic contrasts of which dialogue is capable. He can also help to interpret the play through movement, grouping and *décor*. Character and situation may be emphasized by suitable movements ; the atmosphere of a play can be expressed by its grouping and *décor*; while *décor* also expresses its *locale*.

Interpretation

A third essential in his work is that which we shall call Form. Drama has a form, as well as a content. The content, which is expressed in character and in plot, must be supported by some sort of framework. A picture possesses a subject ; but it also must have composition : a piece of sculpture will have significance as representing some definite object ; but it will also have significance as a decorative shape. In drama, form shows itself through the way in which the plot and the characters are presented; in the relations between the various scenes and the various parts of the scenes. A practised dramatist will contrast his scenes in nature and purpose. He will often sandwich a duologue between two scenes using a greater number of actors, or vice versa. He will follow an emotional scene with one in lighter vein, and precede a dramatic happening with a scene of suspense. In short, he is employing a form of dramatic contrast, not for its own sake alone, but for the sake of creating a pattern which is pleasing for itself.

Form

In transforming the written play into Theatre the producer, of course, expresses this form ; for, once more, the dramatist has bequeathed it to him. But, again, he must do more than this : *he must bring to the performance a " formal" quality in the acting and the movement and the grouping and the* décor. The Form of an actor's performance is that which pleases us apart from what he is saying or doing. It is the " shape " into which he puts his lines. When we listen to a brilliant foreign company acting in a tongue of which we know nothing it is this quality which probably causes us most of our pleasure, for the only purely dramatic impulses we can receive are those which mime and facial expression can communicate. For the rest, we enjoy the sounds of the actors, apart from their words. If those sounds are *systematically* varied in tone, in pitch, in quality and in the pace at which they occur, we are then in fact listening to a sort of " tune " which, though not translatable into musical notation, yet does possess a kind of melodic form. Similarly the *décor* can have its formal decorative quality, as well as its purpose as an indication of *locale* : the grouping can have a constantly changing but constantly attractive significance of its own, quite separate from its dramatic significance ; while the movement of the actors can also have its distinctive value. Once again, we see the value of Dramatic Contrast, which the producer, like the playwright, is here using in no haphazard fashion, but as part of a definite scheme.

The work of the Producer can now be analysed and tabulated as follows :

Intrinsic Factors, which spring solely from the written play itself, and comprise the expression upon the stage of (a) the *Content* of the written play, consisting of its characterization and its plot made dramatic by the author's use of dramatic contrast ; (b) the *Form* of the written play consisting of the author's schematic use of degrees of contrast in his presentation of the characterization and plot for the purposes of design ; and (c) the *Locale* of the play.

These factors are present in even the worst production, for they represent work done by the author himself—work which bad production can scarcely entirely obscure.

Extrinsic Factors, which, while strongly influenced by the written play and suggested by it, yet are the result of the initiative and creative imagination of the producer. These comprise (a) the " Interpretation " of the Content of the written play by means of the fullest use of dramatic contrast in the rendering of dialogue, and in providing significance to movement, grouping and *décor* ; and (b) Form in the performance of the written play, consisting of a schematic use of dramatic contrast in the speaking of dialogue, and in the arrangement of the movements, the grouping and the *décor*.

These are further sub-divided and set forth in the diagram on pages 140 and 141, so that all of the factors necessary to the creation of a piece of Theatre may there be seen at a glance.

The producer's function should now become clear. If, in the performance which he creates, only the intrinsic factors are present, then he is no more successful in his work than the bad orchestral conductor, who is bringing no more to the symphony he is playing than the composer has actually written down in black and white upon his score. Only when he brings the extrinsic factors to bear upon the play does he transform it into a complete piece of Theatre. Only then does he cease to be a mere hack interpreter, and to become a creative artist.

III. DRAMATIC CONTRAST IN PRODUCTION (1)

Variety of Speech

In theory the producer uses Dramatic Contrast in order that the dramatic possibilities of the written play may be further heightened in performance. In practice he uses it to prevent the audience from going to sleep. For there exists in the average audience a collective mental laziness, which causes its attention to wander from what is happening upon the stage, unless its senses are kept continually on the alert. As the price of its complete attention it demands, insatiably and perpetually, *Variety*. Variety in the way the actors speak, in the way they move and in the positions they take up, and variety in the backgrounds before which they perform. Without this variety the most thrilling dramatic situations will lose half their force, and the most effectively written speeches will fall on deaf ears.

For this reason the factor of Dramatic Contrast is perhaps the most important of those with which the producer will have to deal, since no matter how intelligently he may interpret the sense of a play, or how conversant he may be with the psychology of its characters, his work will be wasted utterly if he allows his audience to be bored. From the moment when he first opens his manuscript to begin his work till the fall of the final curtain at his dress rehearsal, he must never once lose sight of this fact.

Under the heading of *Variety of Speech* come those contrasts which are used to make up the *tempo* of a dramatic scene ; contrasts of pitch, intonation, volume, rate of speaking, and the length of interval between the giving and the taking up of a cue : also the use of dramatic pauses, which go to create that tightening and loosening of dramatic tension which constitutes suspense, climax and anti-climax.

Since the primary appeal of the theatre is through the ear, it follows that of all the dramatic contrasts variety of speech is the most important. Consequently almost the first thing that a producer does, when faced with the script of a play for production, is to read it with a view to finding out where he can employ this variety. In doing this he will have to bear in mind certain general principles, *concerning the relation of performance to audience*, which it is as well to enumerate before going any further.

Clarity

1. *Clarity* in performance is a quality of the greatest importance. The audience must be presented with a clear-cut mental image of whatever effect any given portion of a play's dialogue is intended to convey.

2. The perceptive powers of an audience are slow to work. An audience cannot, in fact, react *fully* to more than one effect at a time.

3. For an audience to react fully to any one effect it must be given a period of time during which it can consider that one effect, *to the exclusion of all else*.

4. In practice this means that any line which is intended to convey a particular effect *and which*

it may be of dramatic importance to emphasize, should be followed by a *Dramatic Pause*, in order that the particular effect may have time to sink into the consciousness of the audience.

5. The same applies to any *important* occurrence or piece of action, or piece of stage " business " for which emphasis may be necessary.

6. It therefore follows that in a scene containing a number of lines or speeches calculated to convey *different* effects, and/or containing a number of *different* pieces of action or business, *each* line or speech, and *each* piece of action or business—*if it is worthy of emphasis*—should be separated from its fellow by similar dramatic pauses.

7. The same will apply to whole scenes.   The *transition* between a tragic scene and a lighter scene, or between scenes written in a different method and consequently differing in idea, should be marked by a pause ; otherwise the audience may not obtain a clear-cut idea of each, but a blurred image in which the effects of the scenes merge, and thus counteract each other.

8. The period of time required by an audience to react fully to any effect is greater by far than that required by an individual reacting to the same things in real life.

9. The length of the dramatic pause is to some extent governed by the degree of dramatic value of the line or action or piece of business or scene which precedes it, since the more substance there is to an effect, the longer does it take to sink into the audience.   *Its length may range from a mere taking in of breath to as long as ten seconds.*

Suspense

1. The quality of *Suspense* is of the greatest help in keeping an audience on the alert. Suspense whets an audience's appetite.

2. To create a degree of suspense before an important effect it is only necessary to precede that effect by a pause.

3. The result of the suspense thus created is to emphasize the effect which follows the pause.

4. The length of this preceding pause is to some extent governed by the degree of dramatic importance of the thing to be emphasized.

5. This principle, in a lesser degree, is applied whenever an important line is to be " put over," particularly with lines containing wit and comedy. *In this case the pause employed may last only a second, and the actual period of suspense may take up but a fraction of time.* Yet that tiny degree of suspense will have succeeded in adding point to the line which follows. This method of emphasis is called " pointing " a line.

The Dramatic Pause

It will be seen from these principles that the *Dramatic Pause* is a most valuable instrument in the production of dialogue, for its uses, summed up, are as follows :

(a) It creates clarity by giving an audience time to react to a given dramatic occurrence, whether that occurrence be in words or in action.

(b) It emphasizes a line or an action by means of this time given to the audience.

(c) In the same way it emphasizes the dramatic value of a whole scene.

(*d*) It separates two differing *ideas*.

(*e*) It creates suspense.

(*f*) Through the principle of suspense it is used to
" point " an important line.

Naturally enough, the wise producer will not regard
these principles as rigid rules to be followed slavishly,
for in the theatre there is no such thing as a *rigid*
rule.   Nevertheless, he will find the principles appli-
cable in most cases.

If we now examine the following speech from Act
III of Tchekov's " Uncle Vanya," we may note instances of their use in practice.

> YELENA.   . . . Go to bed !   You bore me.
> VOYNITSKY.   (*Kissing her hand*) My precious . . .
> marvellous one !
> YELENA.   Don't.   This is really hateful.   (*Exit.*)

1 VOYNITSKY.   (*Alone*) She is gone.   Ten years ago
2 I used to meet her at my sister's.   Then she was
3 seventeen and I was thirty-seven.   Why didn't I
4 fall in love with her then and make her an offer ?
5 It might easily have happened then !   And now she
6 would have been my wife.   Yes.   Now we should
7 both have been awakened by the storm ; she would
8 have been frightened by the thunder, I should have
9 held her in my arms and whispered, " Don't be
10 frightened, I am here."   Oh, wonderful thoughts,
11 what happiness : it makes me laugh with delight—
12 but, my God, my thoughts are in a tangle.   Why
13 am I old ?   Why doesn't she understand me ?   Her
14 fine phrases, her lazy morality, her nonsensical lazy
15 theories about the ruin of the world—all that is
16 absolutely hateful to me.   Oh, how I have been
17 cheated !   I adored that Professor, that pitiful gouty
18 invalid, and worked for him like an ox.   Sonya and
19 I squeezed every farthing out of the estate ; we
20 haggled over linseed oil, peas, curds, like greedy

21 peasants ; we grudged ourselves every morsel to save
22 up halfpence and farthings and send him thousands
23 of roubles. I was proud of him and his learning ;
24 he was my life, the breath of my being. All his
25 writings and utterances seemed to me inspired by
26 genius. . . . My God, and now ! Here he is re-
27 tired, and now one can see the sum total of his life.
28 He leaves not one page of work behind him, he is
29 utterly unknown, he is nothing—a soap bubble !
30 And I have been cheated . . . I see it—stupidly
31 cheated. . . .

In seeking opportunities for variety the procedure
is always the same ; namely, to examine the dialogue
most carefully for its *sense*, and to let the variety of
the subject matter suggest the variety appropriate to
its delivery. For instance, the above speech can be
divided, according to its varying significance, into
sections. Each section might be spoken in a different
tone of voice, at a different volume, and at a different
speed. There are two periods of time—the past and
the present : a different tone of voice for each immediately suggests itself. There are a number of different
emotions suggesting different qualities of tone and
rate of speaking. There are transitions from one
thought to another and one mood to another : these
suggest separation by pauses. In fact the speech can
be divided into definite phrases, like a piece of music ;
each phrase being concerned with a different idea
having a tone and rhythm of its own ; yet all being
part of a whole, having its own quality and its own
rhythm.

Now to analyse further :

First, a brief explanation is necessary of the relation
of this speech to the rest of the act. It comes after
the climax of an extremely quick, passionate duologue,

in which Voynitsky (Uncle Vanya) has declared his love for Yelena. Voynitsky, fired with a little too much vodka, has pressed his ardours too far : Yelena, who does not care a fig for him, has repulsed him. She tries to leave the room ; he makes a half-hearted attempt to bar her way, and kisses her again. She shakes him off and makes her exit, and Voynitsky is left alone.

It is now apparent that in addition to the contrasts which lie within the speech, there is the greater contrast of the speech itself, in relation to the scene in which it appears. For the few lines shown of the preceding duologue concern the drama of visible action : the events which occur in it might occur in real life ; the audience are almost in the position of eavesdroppers. But the speech, on the other hand, is a soliloquy, and as such becomes immediately removed from real life ; the author here is deliberately working within the convention that people in a play may communicate their thoughts aloud, and thus give the audience a glimpse of their inner selves. The duologue is concerned with the *surface drama* of the conflict between these two people ; while the speech is concerned with the *drama which lies below the surface*.

Here is an opportunity for a very big dramatic contrast. The divergence of method between the speech and the duologue must be made clear : the mind of the audience, accustomed at first to the realistic convention, must be allowed to proceed smoothly to the acceptance of a non-realistic convention. Unless it is helped to do this by a definite contrast, it will receive a muddled mental image, in which both conventions are mixed up together—and it will also be in the position of trying to take in two effects at the same time.

The contrast will be marked in two ways.   In the first place, by a contrast of speech—as suggested by the sense of the lines.   The passionate, urgent, un- thinking manner of Voynitsky in the duologue will, in the speech, give way to a slower, lower, more ruminative style.   And in the second place it will be marked by a dramatic pause which will separate the two con- ventions of dramatic writing which the author has employed.

Note here the uses of the dramatic pause in practice, for it is shown in all the functions which we have so far described.[1]   It gives the audience *time* to react fully to the dramatic occurrence of Yelena's refusal and exit, and it emphasizes that refusal by means of the time given to the audience ; it emphasizes the dramatic value of the whole preceding scene, and it separates the realistic convention from the non- realistic convention ; it creates suspense in the mind of the audience as to what Voynitsky is going to do next, and through this suspense it lends point and emphasis to the whole of the following speech, because the audience is all the keener for having waited for it.

The pause over, the speech proper begins.   Let us analyse it line by line.   The first three words of line 1 comprise a plain statement of fact, and need only be said in a plain matter-of-fact way.   But they are the first three words of the speech, and therefore they are extremely important in marking the speech contrast which must differentiate these lines from the rest of the scene.   Hence they must be spoken quietly, and slowly :   for Voynitsky's last words have been loud, compelling, and quick.

From here to line 6 the sense is reminiscent, and suggests a soft, brooding tone ;   the first little climax

[1] See page 18.

comes on the words, " And now she would have been my wife," which epitomize the first six lines. It is a pathetic statement, and it sums up a great deal of the pathos of Voynitsky's character. It has, therefore, some dramatic importance, and might be pointed with small dramatic pauses, thus :

And now . . . she would have been my wife. . . . . .

From here till the end of line 11 this idea is developed further : piling image upon image Voynitsky is yearning for what might have been. A rising cadence, an increase of speed and of volume help to build up the picture, and lead to the second climax :

Oh, wonderful thoughts, what happiness !

Again, emphasis for this is necessary, and a pause before and after the line accomplish it. But because this line provides a greater climax, and because the change which follows it is definite indeed, the following pause will need to be a trifle longer than before. Now comes the swift transition from dreams to fact, bringing with it, perhaps, a change of tone to a low, harsh whisper, and a general slowing up of the pace : from here till the middle of line 16 the lines are all the result of the same bitter emotion.

On line 16 comes the biggest dramatic pause of the speech, dividing it into two main sections. Before this point the words all spring from the same idea— the idea of Yelena : they are directly prompted by the preceding scene. But now it is the Professor who becomes the subject of Voynitsky's thoughts. These two utterly different ideas must be well separated ; the pause achieves this, in addition to allowing the audience thoroughly to digest the first half of the speech. The Yelena *motif* is finished ; yet it must not be forgotten—hence the pause to fix it well in the audience's mind.

From line 17 to line 26 the idea behind the words is the same—the idea of the bitterness which can result from a sense of wasted effort. These lines might well be spoken with a certain sameness : yet, lest they should become monotonous, there should be a gradual increase of the emotional intensity behind them. Their effect is cumulative, and they build up to a climax on lines 25 and 26 :

> All his writings and utterances seemed to me inspired by genius.

More could not be said of a man : the picture is complete. The line should be spoken with the broadness of intense irony. And then the picture is shattered with the sudden contrast :

> My God, and now !

At a stroke the mood changes. The final lines sum up to the full Voynitsky's misery, and call for a sombreness of delivery appropriate to the hopelessness they express. The speech ends quietly, as it began, on a note of drabness and monotony.

Tempo, Volume and Pitch

The foregoing analysis has shown examples of variety of pitch, volume, rate of speaking, and of the use of the dramatic pause. It has shown how *tempo* can be varied within a long speech. But it has given no indication of the use of varied *tempo* within a whole scene. In this there is a new factor to be dealt with —*the interval between the giving of a cue and the taking of it up*. This interval is itself capable of variation, and creates a further opportunity for contrast.

It is as well here to state some general principles concerning the *tempo*, the volume, and the pitch of dialogue :

1. In dialogue which is concerned with spontaneous action or spontaneous emotion, and whose drama is therefore on the surface, the interval between the giving of the cues and the taking of them up tends to be so short as to be non-existent ; *and the pace of a scene composed of such dialogue is therefore fast.*

The reason for this is obvious—that the characters who are feeling and acting spontaneously do not need to appear to be giving any great consideration to what they are saying, for they are not ostensibly using their minds.

2. In such surface drama, as the action and the dialogue of the scene become towards its climax less controlled and more spontaneous, the pace and the volume of the dialogue tend to increase, and its pitch to rise.

To anyone who has witnessed a quarrel between two incensed women this is self-evident.

3. Where the drama is below the surface the characters are often speaking lines which are the result of thought, or else speaking lines of which the implications are deeper than the mere significance of the words of which they are composed.   In such cases the pace tends to be slower.

4. Where the drama is below the surface the characters often become more thoughtful, and the dialogue becomes deeper in its implications, as the climax of the scene is approached.   Therefore the pace tends to *decrease* towards the

climax ; and this decrease of pace is often accompanied with a decrease of volume and a falling cadence of pitch.

3 and 4 are but the logical converse of 1 and 2, and are exemplified by the excerpt from " Journey's End " on page 73.

5. A scene's characteristics will be influenced by its most dominant personality. That is, it will tend to be fast or slow, according to the nature of the most important character in it.

The drama of a well-written scene is never entirely submerged or entirely upon the surface : the dramatic level is a constantly changing factor. But in every scene the drama is usually carried by whatever character is dramatically dominant, and it is his nature which will determine the method of treatment that the scene demands.

Let us now examine the following extract from " Othello " (first half of Act V, Scene 2).

A Bedchamber in the Castle. DESDEMONA *in bed asleep.*
A light burning.

Enter OTHELLO.

OTH.	It is the cause, it is the cause, my soul ;
	Let me not name it to you, you chaste stars !
	It is the cause. Yet I'll not shed her blood ;
	Nor scar that whiter skin of hers than snow, 4
	And smooth as monumental alabaster.
	Yet she must die, else she'll betray more men.
	Put out the light, and then put out the light :
	If I quench thee, thou flaming minister, 8
	I can again thy former light restore,
	Should I repent me ; but once put out thy light,
	Thou cunning'st pattern of excelling nature,
	I know not where is that Promethean heat 12

That can thy light relume. When I have pluck'd
the rose,
I cannot give it vital growth again,
It needs must wither : I'll smell it on the tree.
(*Kisses her.*)
O balmy breath, that dost almost persuade 16
Justice to break her sword ! One more, one
more.
Be thus when thou art dead, and I will kill thee,
And love thee after. One more, and this the
last :
So sweet was ne'er so fatal. I must weep, 20
But they are cruel tears ; this sorrow's heavenly ;
It strikes where it doth love. She wakes.

DES. Who's there ? Othello ?
OTH.   Ay, Desdemona.
DES. Will you come to bed, my lord ?   24
OTH. Have you pray'd to-night, Desdemona ?
DES.   Ay, my lord.
OTH. If you bethink yourself of any crime
Unreconciled as yet to Heaven and grace,
Solicit for it straight.   28
DES. Alas ! my lord, what may you mean by that ?
OTH. Well, do it, and be brief ; I will walk by :
I would not kill thy unprepared spirit ;
No ; Heaven forfend ! I would not kill thy
soul.   32
DES. Talk you of killing ?
OTH.   Ay, I do.
DES.   Then Heaven
Have mercy on me !
OTH.   Amen ! with all my heart.
DES. If you say so, I hope you will not kill me.
OTH. Hum !   36
DES. And yet I fear you ; for you are fatal then
When your eyes roll so. Why I should fear I
know not,
Since guiltiness I know not ; but yet I feel I fear.

OTH.   Think on thy sins.

DES.   They are loves I bear to you. 40

OTH.   Ay, and for that thou diest.

DES.   That death's unnatural that kills for loving.
         Alas ! Why gnaw you so your nether lip ?
         Some bloody passion shakes your very frame ; 44
         These are portents, but yet, I hope, I hope
         They do not point on me.

OTH.   Peace, and be still !

DES.   I will so. What's the matter ?

OTH.   That handkerchief which I so lov'd and gave
             thee   48
         Thou gav'st to Cassio.

DES.   No, by my life and soul !
         Send for the man, and ask him.

OTH.   Sweet soul, take heed,
         Take heed of perjury ; thou'rt on thy death-bed.

DES.   Ay, but not yet to die ;   52

OTH.   Yes, presently ;
         Therefore confess thee freely of thy sin ;
         For to deny each article with oath
         Cannot remove nor choke the strong conception
         That I do groan withal. Thou art to die. 56

DES.   The Lord have mercy upon me !

OTH.   I say, amen.

DES.   And have you mercy too ! I never did
         Offend you in my life ; never lov'd Cassio
         But with such general warranty of Heaven 60
         As I might love ; I never gave him token.

OTH.   By Heaven, I saw my handkerchief in's hand.
         O perjur'd woman ! Thou dost stone my heart,
         And mak'st me call what I intend to do   64
         A murder, which I called a sacrifice :
         I saw the handkerchief.

DES.   He found it then ;
         I never gave it him ; send for him hither ;
         Let him confess a truth.   68

OTH.   He hath confess'd.

DES.   What, my lord?
OTH.   That he hath us'd thee.
DES.   How?   Unlawfully?
OTH.   Ay.
DES.   He will not say so.
OTH.   No; his mouth is stopped:
            Honest Iago hath ta'en order for't.   72
DES.   O! My fear interprets. What! is he dead?
OTH.   Had all his hairs been lives, my great revenge
            Had stomach for them all.
DES.   Alas! he is betray'd and I undone.   76
OTH.   Out, strumpet! weep'st thou for him to my face?
DES.   O! banish me. my lord, but kill me not!
OTH.   Down, strumpet!
DES.   Kill me to-morrow; let me live to-night!   80
OTH.   Nay, if you strive——
DES.   But half an hour!
OTH.   Being done, there is no pause.
DES.   But while I say one prayer!
OTH.   It is too late.   (*He smothers her.*)
EMILIA.   (*Within*) My lord, my lord! What ho! My
            lord, my lord!   84
OTH   What noise is this? Not dead? Not yet quite
            dead?
            I that am cruel am yet merciful;
            I would not have thee linger in thy pain.
            So, so.
EMILIA.   (*Within*) What ho! My lord, my lord!
OTH.   Who's there? 88

Now in the above scene it will be obvious that it is
Othello who is the dominant character. Although
there are moments when the drama is below the
surface, yet the predominating emotions are passion,
jealousy, revenge—all of which are the result of un-
bridled, unthinking *spontaneous feeling.*

Therefore the pace and volume of the scene must
increase, and its general pitch must rise, until the

climax—the point where Othello smothers Desdemona
—is reached.[1]　Obviously, to give an impression of increasing speed and volume one must begin slowly and
quietly : thus the opening speech of the scene will be
soft, and deliberate.

If we examine this opening speech we find that
Shakespeare himself had such a magnificent feeling for
dramatic contrast that his lines could not possibly be
spoken in any other way.　For the whole of this soliloquy is the expression of the subterranean conflict within
Othello's mind.　If it is spoken quietly and slowly,
the tragic irony of its words will create an effect of
brooding ominousness : the comparative calmness here
will seem to foreshadow a storm to come.

With the awakening of Desdemona comes the first
big contrast—marked, of course, by a pause ; for (a)
the end of the soliloquy marks the transition from the
unrealistic convention of spoken thought, to the comparative realism of dialogue, and also the transition
from submerged drama to surface drama ; (b) the
effect of the soliloquy must have time to sink into
the audience ; (c) the audience is on tenterhooks to
see and hear what is going to happen the moment
Desdemona achieves consciousness, therefore suspense
here will increase their excitement.　The pause will be
taken up with business—Desdemona stirring, then
opening her eyes, then sitting up, and so forth.

Now come opportunities for contrasts of voice and
of pace.　These would depend, of course, upon the
producer's interpretation of the lines.　A possible interpretation is the following :

Desdemona's voice is frail, bewildered : Othello's
words are harsh, definite.　She senses something
strange in his manner : therefore she is not quick on

[1] See page 25.

her cues at first, but pauses slightly as she tries to comprehend the situation. On the other hand, Othello's grim determination makes him quick, and his answers are rapped out smartly on the cues. On line 25 he asks her whether she has prayed : a new note here creeps into her answer—uneasiness. Their mode of speaking is reversed : Othello is playing cat and mouse ; he speaks slowly on his cues, and Desdemona on line 29 quickly presses for an explanation.

It is from this point that the dramatic intensity of the scene increases until the climax is reached : the *tempo* must therefore quicken, which means that the *general* pace, the *general* volume and the *general* intensity of the emotion expressed must all be heightened increasingly un†il the smothering takes place. But within this general speeding up of the *tempo* various contrasts still exist, as suggested by the sense. For instance, the lines :

OTH.   No ; Heaven forfend ! I would not kill thy soul. 32

              Short pause, or breath.

DES.   Talk you of killing ?
OTH.   Ay, I do.

              Short pause, or breath.

DES.   Then Heaven
Have mercy upon me !

The two short pauses, although the time they take up is infinitesimal—a mere gasp or quick intaking of breath would suffice—are yet of great importance. For the line " I would not kill thy soul " is full of significance in what it does *not* say : it demands, therefore, an emphasis appropriate to its importance, in other words, " pointing." And the effect of those words on Desdemona is important, since it is the first time in the scene that killing is mentioned. The audience must have time, first to realize the import of the line, and secondly to realize its import for Desdemona : also Desdemona must have time to *express that effect by her acting*. The same applies to the line " Ay, I do." The audience must have time to realize the terrible significance of these words ; then when Desdemona makes her pathetic appeal to Heaven, the audience's feeling for her is increased by the extra dramatic value the words have received.

From here onward Othello speaks quicker and quicker on his cues : for he is mad and uncontrollable in the grip of his jealousy ; his words are unthinking, impetuous, and pour out in a torrent. Desdemona, on the other hand, though she too must speed up as the general pace of the scene increases, must yet here and there still contrive to give the impression of hesitancy ; for she is thinking hard, fighting for her life, arguing, extenuating, explaining. Moreover, she is repeatedly reeling under the shock of accusations which are to her incredible, and which must momentarily strike her dumb and helpless with amazement. When Othello says : " The handkerchief which I so lov'd and gave thee thou gav'st to Cassio " (line 48), Desdemona simply does not know what to say : but after a little pause—a gasp of fevered surprise—she returns once more to her defence and her denials.

Again, when she speaks of Cassio's innocence :

DES.   I never gave it him ; send for him hither ;
　　　　Let him confess a truth.　　　　　　　　　68
OTH.   He hath confess'd.

Short pause, or breath.

DES.   What, my lord ?

Desdemona *knows* that Cassio's confession would vindicate her. Her words strike almost a faint note of triumph—then, momentarily, she is struck speechless by the grim twist of Othello's reply : " He *hath* confess'd " The world must seem to fall from under her feet—this is the last statement she expected to hear. But in a second she returns to the struggle, though now she must realize that no matter what she says, Othello will not believe her.

Again, after Othello's line :

> No ; his mouth is stopped :
> Honest Iago hath ta'en order for't.   72

Two tiny pauses—mere breaths—for " pointing " are needed here. First, before and after the word " Honest Iago." " Honest Iago " must be emphasized just a little, for Shakespeare's masterly use of this phrase, *at this particular point*, sums up more trenchantly that monster's villainy than any fuller description could possibly do. And, secondly, a pause is needed after the completion of the line, to allow the statement that Cassio has been killed to create its full effect, both upon the audience, and upon Desdemona.

This latter pause gives Desdemona opportunity for a valuable change of vocal pitch. We have seen how, as an emotional scene rises towards its climax, it increases in speed and in volume, and rises in pitch.[1] It is obvious, however, that no matter how slowly or how quietly or how low in pitch it may begin, there is not sufficient range in the human voice to maintain this increase throughout the entire scene, even if this were desirable (which, since we are seeking opportunities for contrasts, it is not). Therefore opportunities must be found for the performer to indulge in a sort

[1] See page 25.

of " breather," in which his energies are recouped, and after which he pursues his course towards the climax with renewed vigour. When these breathers are taken in the right places the resultant contrasts are themselves dramatic in effect, so that the general effect of an unbroken sweep of dramatic intensity towards the inevitable climax is not actually lost at all, although the pace, the pitch, and the volume may have all momentarily lapsed.

That is what has happened throughout this scene. The opportunities for pauses which we have discovered are all " breathers." In each case they have occasioned a change of pitch and of volume as well, of course, as a change of pace.

Now, after Othello's statement that Cassio has been dealt with comes the biggest " breather " of them all. The dialogue from the line : " What, my lord ? " (line 69) to " No ; his mouth is stopped ; " (line 71) is all spoken with rising inflexions, and with an increase of volume and pace. That dialogue is all concerned with a single idea—the idea of Desdemona's supposed unfaithfulness. Suddenly, a new idea is presented—the idea of Cassio's supposed death. The following pause, therefore, in addition to pointing the idea, is also giving the audience time to react to this sudden change. It is further giving time for Desdemona to do so. Then, when she does react to it, she must obviously react to it as to a *new* turn in the situation. Hence, when she speaks, she speaks with a different voice. For a moment, all fear for herself is gone : it is of Cassio only that she thinks. Her line : " O ! my fear interprets ! " could therefore be low and deep in quality. Othello's answering words, too, are apart from the general tenor of the scene ; there is consequently every reason for a change of voice here. Both these lines are in the nature of an interpolation. By being spoken in a different way from those in the context, they are " lifted out " of the scene, and emphasized as such. The resulting momentary dropping of the pace, volume and pitch allows both Othello and Desdemona to ease off, as it were. before going all out for the final lap, when once more the pace is taken up with the lines :

Alas ! he is betray'd and I undone.

From now, till the moment where she is smothered, there is no holding back the relentless sweep of the scene : it must rise in pitch, and increase in volume and in pace, as Othello's emotions become more and more uncontrollable. Crescendo—and then the tension snaps : the deed is done. There follows—*not yet* the frantic shrieking of Emilia—but a long, a very long, dramatic pause.

For it must be realized, that although Desdemona does speak a few words later on in the scene before she actually dies, yet, as far as the emotional reactions of the audience are concerned, the dramatic value of her death exists in the act which kills her, and in the few moments which follow that act. These moments form the grand climax of the play : therefore the pause at this juncture is of the very greatest dramatic importance, illustrating, as it does, every one of its functions :

(*a*) The murder of Desdemona forms the climax of the play, and is the most important single act of the play. The audience must therefore be given time to react fully to it and to realize completely its horror and its tragedy. It must be " mentally digested."

(*b*) Through the consequent opportunity for mental digestion the dramatic value of the murder is heightened and the murder itself consequently brought into relief.

(c) The pause, in addition to giving the audience time to react fully to the murder, gives them time to react fully to all that has gone before it. The entire effect of the scene is therefore heightened.

(d) The pause is helping to separate two differing ideas : in the first place, it tides over the transition between the effect of the murder and the effect of Emilia's voice (which introduces a new *motif* into the scene) ; and in the second it tides over the transition between two different emotions in the audience itself. If, as suggested by the text, Emilia were to speak immediately after the smothering of Desdemona, the dramatic effect of the smothering would be confused and blurred by the sudden introduction of a *different* effect. The same " blur " would occur in the emotions of the audience. For, since the murder, those emotions have undergone a change. During the scene which leads up to the smothering, the preponderant emotion is one of pity for Desdemona ; but that pity is so submerged by suspense—the fear of what Othello is going to do—that when Othello actually carries out his threat and smothers her, the resulting snapping of the tension brings with it almost a sense of relief. And with that relief there surges through the audience the *pure* emotion of pity, unclouded by any other feeling of suspense or otherwise. Therefore, from the moment just before the murder to the moment just after it, the emotions of the audience have progressed from a superflux of suspense to a superflux of pity. And the dramatic pause must be there to tide over that change, otherwise the most important feeling of pure pity will never get the chance to make itself felt.

(e) The pause is also helping to create suspense as to what will happen next.

(f) Therefore, when Emilia finally does speak, her

words have an added emphasis by reason of their contrast with silence.

(g) Additionally, the pause serves for dramatic contrast alone : the quick violence of the preceding scene seeming to demand the relief of silence.

(h) The pause is a valuable " breather." The rest of the play, after Emilia's entrance, remains somewhat on the same note of dramatic accusations, recriminations and disclosures—all " surface drama," which permits of scarcely any lessening of the pace until the very end. The pause will allow the actor playing Othello to start again at the bottom of his range ; and it will permit the audience to relax for a few moments, before their attention is once more held concentrated till the final curtain.

Every one of these things must happen during this pause. They cannot happen at once. Hence the pause here must be *long*—from, say, five to ten seconds. But it must not be a " dead " pause. The actor must convey, with his eyes and his facial expression, all that will be going on in Othello's mind at this moment. He will, however, take care to keep still : otherwise the audience will be distracted by his movement, and the tension caused by the pause will be broken.

As we have seen, variety of speech is easily suggested by the dialogue itself ; and it is as well that this should be so, for if the producer is to allow an author's words to come through to the audience in their true meaning, he must not indulge in contrasts which have no relation to the sense. Some plays, however, are so written that the suggestions for variety are not obvious. Modern plays, of a certain naturalistic kind, often possess dialogue which might be spoken in dozens of different ways and still keep their same significance. In these cases, the producer must use his own judgment in allocating his emphases. Faced with two characters who seem in print to speak with a tiresome similarity, he can make one speak habitually slower than the other : if he has to tackle a scene in which two characters both have lengthy and consecutive emotional speeches to make—a common fault with young authors—he can make one of them speak in a high pitch and rather loudly, while letting the other speak in a low tone and somewhat quietly. Provided he does not, as Hamlet said to the First Player, " o'erstep the modesty of Nature," and give more value to a word or a line than its meaning would seem reasonably to warrant, he is not likely to go wrong if he remembers that, *under no circumstances should the dialogue of a play continue for long in the same manner of delivery.*

IV. DRAMATIC CONTRAST (2)

Movement

VARIETY of Speech is not enough by itself to capture
and hold the attention of the audience. No matter
how brilliant may be the part given to an actor, or
how well that part may be spoken, unless the performance is broken up with plenty of movement it
will lose much of its dramatic force.

But stage movement, unless it is properly handled,
can become a most dangerous thing; for, badly
manipulated, it will often distract the audience from
more important considerations. It is therefore essential for the producer to know exactly why every movement in the production under his control is taking
place. For this purpose it is valuable to classify the
various types of stage movement under their various
headings.

All stage movement can be considered from three
different points of view. First, from that of the
producer, who directs and controls it : second, from
the point of view of the audience which watches it ;
and third, from the point of view of the character
who, ostensibly, makes it.

From the producer's viewpoint, every movement
that takes place during a performance may have been
affected by one or all of three influences : (a) The
desire of the producer to move his characters about

the stage in such a manner that, by the ever-changing groups which they present, a series of contrasts are created ; (b) *The necessity for each character to appear to move as if he had a will of his own in a smooth and natural manner ;* (c) The desire of the producer to use movement, as far as is practicable, as an aid to dramatic expression.

From the audience's viewpoint there are, quite simply, two kinds of stage movement : (a) Movement of intrinsic dramatic value ; (b) Movement of no intrinsic dramatic value.

From the point of view of the character himself, movement is again of two kinds : (a) Conscious Movement ; (b) Unconscious Movement.

It is under the heading, Conscious and Unconscious Movement, that stage movement is most easily examined.

Conscious movement is, from the point of view of the producer, the easiest type of movement with which to seek variety. For he must always seek an *excuse* for the movements of his characters, and conscious movement provides that excuse in an ostensible reason within the mind of the character himself, such as the opening or closing of a door, making an exit, fetching a cigarette, etc. Often these excuses are already provided by the dramatist, who has probably incorporated certain essential movements into his script. More still will be found by the producer, who will comb the dialogue for appropriate opportunities. Such *concrete* reasons for movement are, however, comparatively rare : there is patently a limit to the number of doors to be shut and the number of fires to be poked. Hence the producer must look beyond them for subtler excuses—excuses which are psychological rather than practical. Let us take, for example, the following piece of dialogue :

MASON (*by door, down-stage* R.). You mean . . . you've betrayed us ?

HARKER (*by window, up-stage* L.). If you like to call it that.

(HARKER *shrugs his shoulders.* MASON *loses control of himself.*)

MASON. You filthy lying swine ! By God, I might have known it . . . what's going to become of us now !

(*He rattles the door handle. The door is locked.*)

Help ! Help ! For God's sake . . .

HARKER (*quietly*). Shut up, you fool, they're asleep. . . . . . And . . . Mason . . . if you open your mouth again . . . (*he taps his revolver*) we'll settle accounts right here.

MASON (*trembling*). I'm sorry . . . I'll keep quiet.

HARKER. I thought you would. . . . And now, let's talk of something more pleasant, shall we ?

Suppose we examine this from the point of view of the producer seeking movement. Suppose that, for some reason or other, our problem is to reverse the positions of Harker and Mason, so as to bring the former to Down Stage Right, by the door, and the latter, say to Down Stage Left, by the fireplace. This is what we must do :

First, we note the characters of Harker and Mason —or such small evidence concerning them as this small piece of dialogue gives us. We see that Mason is frightened, hysterical and uncontrolled, while Harker is the very reverse, strong, quiet and dominant. We see also that Harker has some sort of hold over Mason. We see, further, that from the point of view of vocal contrasts there are numerous opportunities for valuable dramatic pauses (already marked in the dialogue, for the sake of clarity, by a succession of dots). We may note particularly the pause in the line:

And, Mason . . . if you open your mouth again, we'll settle accounts right here.

The line and the business of tapping the revolver constitute an effective and dramatic threat. The words " And, Mason," if spoken quietly and ominously, are a sort of prelude to that threat : they form a signpost to the audience—and to Mason—telling both that the threat is to come. Therefore the pause [1] after these words is effective because it creates a period of suspense between the implication of the threat and its actual statement, thus emphasizing the effect of the threat when it is made.

Suppose, during this pause, we make Harker cross over deliberately to Mason. Is this justifiable ? Does it help to form an actual dramatic contrast ? Yes, since for three or four speeches the characters have been in the same positions and our problem is to move them. Is it natural ? Yes, because Harker is intimidating Mason : he is making a conscious movement towards him for the psychological reason that he knows this will help to frighten him. Every step he makes towards his cringing companion will help to reduce Mason to that state of subjection which his next words about settling accounts will finally complete. Is it an aid to a fuller dramatic expression of the scene ? Yes, for the move at this point is amplifying the effect of the dramatic pause in which it is made, *because it is allowing the pause to continue for a longer period than would be possible without it.* In theory,

[1] See page 18.

the longer is the pause, the greater is the suspense, and the greater the consequent emphasis on the succeeding line.[1] In practice, owing to the notorious tendency of the audience to wander from the point unless something is happening on the stage, the pause could not *unaided* last more than two seconds without the audience losing interest. But with the help of Harker's movement, which fastens the attention of the audience upon him during the entire period of his moving, the pause here may last as long as six seconds or more, with a consequent great increase of suspense and resulting emphasis.

So far, so good. Our next problem is to get Mason away from the door and over to the other side of the stage.

Harker makes his threat His eyes never leave Mason's, as both men are standing by the door. Mason apologizes abjectly. Harker, fixing him with a steely eye, says grimly : " I thought you would." There is here another dramatic pause. Mason, as we know, is weak, easily frightened. He cannot bear the other's gaze. Slowly, he edges away from him ; and then, more quickly in his fear, he moves to the fireplace and sits down. The movement here is natural enough for it is a clear expression of Mason's own character and the unpleasantness of Mason's situation. And it is an aid to dramatic expression because it is again amplifying the effect of a dramatic pause [2]—the pause which punches home the effect of the sarcasm in the line " I thought you would " and which also tides [2] over the transition between the underlying seriousness of that line and the lightness of " And now, let's talk of something else " which immediately follows it. The positions are now reversed, and our problem is solved.

[1] See page 18.   [2] See pages 18, 19.

It will be noted that both these conscious movements, being *aids to dramatic expression*,[1] are *movements which possess* [1] *intrinsic dramatic value*. For they constitute each in themselves a dramatic effect. Therefore, though they each help to emphasize the pauses in which they occur, the converse is also true, that the pauses [2] are essential in order that the movements themselves may be emphasized. We may now lay down the following principles concerning movement.

1. Where a movement is itself of dramatic significance it should *not* be accompanied by dialogue.

The corollary is also true, that :

2. Where the dialogue is of particular dramatic significance, it should *not* be accompanied by movement.

It therefore follows that :

3. Where the dialogue is *not* of particular dramatic significance, it *may* be accompanied by movement.

and that :

4. Where the movement is *not* of particular dramatic significance, it *may* be accompanied by dialogue.

These principles are but the logical outcome of those of Clarity, where it is laid down that an audience can only take in and react to *one effect at a time*. If we glance again at the Harker-Mason duologue we can easily find examples of their working. Mason's first line is obviously a line of considerable dramatic significance, in which the idea of betrayal is put forward for the first time : it would therefore be wrong for either Harker or Mason to make a movement here. Similarly Harker's answer is of dramatic importance, since it is the key to his attitude to the situation ;

[1] See pages 39, 40.　　　[2] See pages 18, 19.

there can be no movement here, either. But let us examine Mason's next speech : " You filthy lying swine . . . ," etc. Here it is not the actual words of the speech that have significance, but rather the way in which those words are spoken. The intended effect is hysteria, terror, impotent rage ; and *any* words expressing such emotions would do just as well as those which are written. Therefore *these words are not of dramatic importance*, and if the producer wished Mason to move during their delivery, he would be entitled to give him a blustering movement to Harker and then back to the door, speaking the entire time.

Such a movement would not, however, possess any intrinsic dramatic significance, for in no way would it enhance the effect of either lines or situation. It would only be made for the reason that the producer, for his own purposes, wished to shift Mason's position at this particular point. But it illustrates a case where unimportant movement might permit of concurrent speaking, and, conversely, where unimportant lines might permit of concurrent movement. As a rule, conscious movements of this kind, made for a *psychological reason only tend to be the movements of dramatic value rather than otherwise*. For there is no particular point in the tentative movement for Mason outlined above : the sense of the dialogue is quite sufficient to show the blustering, whining nature of the man.

On the other hand, those conscious movements which are of a *practical* nature may or may not be of dramatic importance, according to the nature of the context. A character may move to shut a door because it is a link in the plot that the audience should see that door shut. Or he may simply shut it because the producer finds it inconvenient to leave it open, or wishes to move his character to another part of the stage, or some other equally trivial reason. In the first case he will shut that door during a pause in the dialogue, so that the attention of the audience may concentrate upon him. In the second case he will shut it unobtrusively while the dialogue is in progress, *but taking care that the dialogue, whose clarity of expression he is thus hindering, is of no particular dramatic importance.*

In the making of entrances and exits, the rule will be the same. The producer must decide which effect is of the most importance—the *entrance* or *exit* of a character, or the *lines* with which he makes his entrance and exit. If the entrance matters most, he will *not speak until he has entered* and taken up his position on the stage ; if the exit must claim attention, he will speak his farewell lines *before* moving to the door. If, on the other hand, the dramatic emphasis is on the opening or closing *lines* of a character, he will speak at the door, before coming fully on to the stage, and again at the door before leaving it ; (having prepared his exit by getting to the door at a suitable previous spot in the dialogue). Again, if neither the movement nor the dialogue is particularly important, and if the effect desired is simply one of casual, inconsequent conversation, the character will actually speak his lines as he comes on or goes off.

Unconscious Movement.

The bulk of the movements employed in a performance are those of which the characters making them are ostensibly unconscious. In the producer's perpetual search for variety, they provide him with almost limitless freedom of choice, as well as with his greatest source of danger. For there is often no apparent reason for an unconscious movement, and it may therefore so easily seem unnatural and distracting. But, whether there is an ostensible reason for it or not, the *unconscious movement must yet be made in such a way that the characters move naturally and plausibly*.[1]

Unconscious movements often possess no dramatic value whatsoever, and of these little need be said. They are only permissible if they can pass unnoticed, and a producer is entitled to use just as many as he is able to get away with. Needless to say, he will not be able to get away with a great many, because, in order to avoid distraction, he can only employ them in those parts of the play where the dialogue is of practically no importance. As long as the characters confine themselves to observing that it is a fine day, and that the nights are drawing in, so long will the producer be able to let them move aimlessly with impunity. But even then he must take care not to overdo it, for a cumulation of meaningless movements will ultimately be certain to become distracting.

But sometimes there appears another type of unconscious movement, whose effect is cumulative, not particularized, and of whose significance the audience may be dimly and subconsciously aware. A character may make a movement of no apparent meaning, but, as he continues to make it with less or greater frequency, he may ultimately register by it some such effect as impatience, nervousness, apprehension, joy, etc.

In seeking opportunities for using this movement the producer will get his inspiration from the implications of the dialogue. He will often use it to give variety to long speeches, as, for example, in Hamlet's " To be, or not to be," soliloquy. However well this speech may be spoken, the audience will tend to lose their keenest interest unless some sort of movement is pro-

[1] See pages 39, 40.

vided with it. There is here no opportunity for conscious movement, and no occasion for movement of any particular dramatic value ; yet the groping thoughtfulness of the speech does allow for a vague wandering about on the part of Hamlet which would be perfectly natural to him. One movement here would mean nothing at all, but the cumulative effect of two or three movements would act as an indication of Hamlet's state of mind. It is perhaps scarcely necessary to add, that since every word of this speech is of vital significance, such movements should only occur during pauses between the lines.

Movement of this kind is of great assistance in the expression of character, as we shall later see, in the chapter dealing with Interpretation. It is enough to say here that it provides to the greatest degree those variations of position which are necessary for dramatic contrast, and that, consequently, the producer in seeking opportunities for it, must delve deeply down into the characterization of the play.

There is some relation between the pace of a movement and the pace of the dialogue which is associated with it. This is largely a matter for feeling and common sense. Slow dialogue will usually demand slowness of movement, and fast dialogue fast movement. This is not always the case, however, with movements which are consciously made. If a conscious movement, of dramatic importance, is to be emphasized, there will obviously be virtue in deliberately breaking its rhythmic relation to the dialogue, for the sake of the resulting contrast. This is what has happened in the Harker-Mason duologue. Harker's *slow* move towards Mason is of great dramatic importance, and its effect is heightened by the contrast which it makes with the speedy dialogue before and after it. But the more unconscious a movement becomes, the more will its *tempo* have to accord with that of the dialogue through which it is made. In the Hamlet soliloquy, for instance, it would be absurd for Hamlet to move other than slowly and thoughtfully.

For the purpose of analysing stage movement, we have had to fit it into categories. The reader will, however, realize that such categories must not be taken to constitute rigid definitions. Just as no scene is completely composed of "submerged drama," or completely spontaneous, no movement is always entirely conscious or unconscious. But, according as it leans towards the one category or the other, the producer will know how and where it should be employed.

In addition, for the purposes of illustration, all the movements we have instanced have been those where a character has actually progressed from one part of the stage to another. It is as well, therefore, to add that the term " Movement " includes everything that an actor may do with his body. The slightest gesture, or turn of the head, or shifting of the feet may have in the right circumstances the very greatest significance : consequently all the principles which apply to the broader movements will also apply to them. An actor who swings his head, or sways from the hips, or fidgets, is just as capable of distracting an audience, as one who does so by walking about through important pieces of dialogue.

Finally, let two pieces of advice sum up this chapter :

As far as is possible, all movements in a performance should have some sort of significance, or some sort of excuse.

For the rest, which have neither, let them be such as to pass unnoticed.

V. DRAMATIC CONTRAST (3)

Grouping and Décor

Grouping. We have seen how and where a producer may use movement in working out the performance of a play, and we have seen how by the various kinds of movement dramatic contrast may be obtained. We have treated movement as an end : we have here to regard it as a means to another end ; for just as the audience must be kept continually alive by variety of movement and speech, so must its senses be continually stimulated by the variety of grouping which movement makes possible.

In seeking for the varied arrangements of the characters which the performance of a play demands, inspiration must come, as with the voice and movement contrasts, from the sense of the dialogue. Just as important lines may be pointed by a pause or a certain inflexion or a movement, so a dramatic situation may be emphasized by the relative positions of the actors on the stage.

This emphasis consists in so arranging the grouping that the positions of the characters are always consistent with their relative dramatic importance ; with the predominant character of the scene in the dominating position, and the next most important character in the position of secondary importance, and so on. As the dramatic emphasis shifts from one character to another, so must the grouping rearrange itself in such a way that he who dominates the play at any given moment also dominates the scene.

Now a most important instrument of the actor is not only his voice, but his face. One has only to listen to a good actor delivering a soliloquy in the dark to realize that, without the wealth of expression of which the mouth and eyes are capable, the best voice in the world is no match for the audience's capacity for sleep. Therefore the most effective dramatic position for an actor on the stage is that position where the audience can not only hear him best, but can best see every portion of his face and body. For the delivering of a soliloquy, this position is naturally as far " downstage " as is practicable, that is to say, as near to the footlights (and therefore to the audience) as will permit the lighting system yet to make the actor visible. From time to time, in order to avoid monotony, he would show his profile to the audience : but mostly he would so appear to them that, while not facing them directly and squarely (this aspect can soon become uninteresting even with the most prepossessing countenances), he is yet allowing them *to see both his eyes*. For the eyes are the source of all conviction in acting, and the actor who, by playing too much in profile, does not utilize them to the fullest degree, will not be able to hold his audience for long.

Now suppose this soliloquy becomes a duologue. Two actors together on the stage would naturally tend to face each other as they talk, and in so doing would play in profile and lose a proportion of their potential effectiveness. In a short scene, or in a scene of comparatively slight significance, where the characters have perhaps already been introduced and explained

to the audience, this would not matter. But with a
longer scene, with important characters and important
lines, such a weakening of the dramatic effect would
be a serious fault. In such a case it is the producer's
task to decide at which parts of the scene one character
and one sequence of speeches becomes more important
than the other character and another sequence of
speeches. And, as each character be-
Dramatic
Domination comes dominant in the scene, he will
have to be placed in the most effective
and dominant position; that is, he will have to
stand " up-stage " of his fellow—farther towards the
back of the stage—so that his face is turned more
fully towards the audience. If then the dialogue so
develops that the dramatic importance shifts from
one character to the other, the positions will have to
be reversed—by a suitable movement, at a suitable
point—so that the character with the most important
lines to speak is always " up-stage " of the character
of lesser importance. The effectiveness thus gained
is, of course, always at the expense of the lesser
character. But this does not matter, for—remembering that an audience can only take in one thing
at a time—it is always desirable to concentrate
attention in one direction only, and that the most
important.

The effect of this arrangement is twofold. *The
up-stage character is emphasized by reason of his greater
effectiveness. And, because of this emphasis, he not
only dominates the scene, but appears also to dominate
the other character, who, handicapped by his position,
becomes, apparently, subordinate to him.* We may call
this principle that of *dramatic domination.*

When more than two characters are on the

stage at the same time another factor comes into play, due to a peculiar characteristic of the human eye.

Normally the eye of an audience will rest upon whatever character in a performance happens to be speaking at a given moment. But, like the attention of an audience, it has a tendency **Stage " Focal Point "** to wander. It tends to wander in a definite direction, to seek out a focal point somewhere on the stage, and there to rest. If a character's lines are of sufficient dramatic interest and are well enough spoken, they will serve to keep the eye of the audience upon that character. But if at any moment there is a lapse of dramatic tension, off goes the eye on its wanderings until it finds that focal point. To guard against this, the producer must so arrange his grouping that the position of his dominant character and that of the focal point coincide.

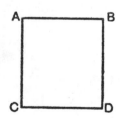
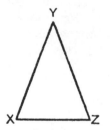

FIG. 1.

Above we see a rectangle ABCD and a triangle XYZ. If the eye is allowed casually to regard the rectangle it will not tend to rest upon a definite point, but will idly follow the lines round and round until it is weary. On the other hand, if it regards the triangle it will tend to be led up the sides XY

c

and ZY to the apex Y, where it will tend to rest. If we now break the straight line on top of the rectangle to form a triangle thus :

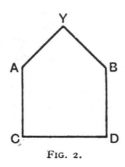

FIG. 2.

the eye will this time be led up the sides CA and DB to rest on the apex Y.

Evidently the triangle possesses a focal point for the eye, while the rectangle does not.

Next, let us suppose a series of triangles, each larger than the other :

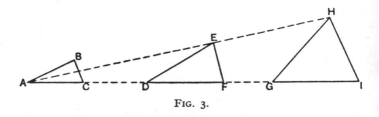

FIG. 3.

In this case the eye is led first to the apex of the smallest triangle ABC, then to that of the larger DEF, and finally to that of the greatest, GHI. And the apex H of the greatest triangle forms the ultimate focal point, since it is the apex of the greater triangle AHI, here drawn with a dotted line.

Now an audience, faced with a stage picture, will pick on certain dominant features—such as chairs, windows, or the characters themselves—and will subconsciously form of them similar triangles, *to the apices of which its eye will tend to wander*. Hence it is always possible by a suitable arrangement of these features to place the focal point exactly where the producer wishes. Suppose that we number the corners of the three triangles of the previous figure, and that we imagine them to be characters upon a stage :

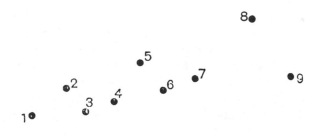

Characters number 2, 5 and 8 are standing in the positions of greatest emphasis. The eye is led to 2, and then to 5, and finally to 8. 2 is in the dominant position as regards 1 and 3 ; 5 dominates 4 and 6, while 8 dominates 7 and 9. But character number 8 is also dominating all the others, for he is not only in the position of dramatic domination, but also in the focal point of the triangle formed by 1 8 9.

Now this principle of the focal point will often provide an exception to the principle of dramatic domination, for it shows us that the dominating position is not necessarily always that which is far-thest up-stage :

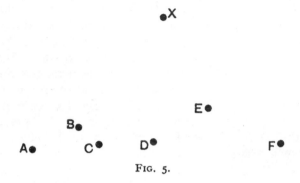

Fig. 5.

In the above figure the position which is *apparently* of the greatest dominance is that of X. But it will be noticed that X is farther away from the rest of the characters than any of them are from each other : hence X does not readily associate himself with any imaginary scheme of triangles. As we see in Fig. 6—

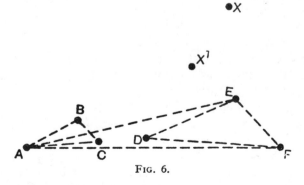

Fig. 6.

he is " out of the scene," while the rest of the characters group themselves easily into triangles ABC and DEF. E is consequently the figure of greatest emphasis, for he has some sort of association with the other characters and at the same time he forms the apex of the large triangle AEF. On the other hand, we have only to make X drop down-stage a little to X^1, so that the distance between X^1 and the rest is not markedly greater than that of the rest between each other, and we find that X^1 easily forms the apex of the triangle ABX^1EF, and so is now in the dominating position.

This suggests that the acting area of the stage may be divided into zones of varying degrees of effectiveness. Beginning with the down-stage portion we find that the farther we go up-stage the more dominating become the positions, until a point is reached, about two-thirds of the distance towards the back wall, where there is a rapid decrease, till the very back of the stage ceases to have any importance at all.

The value of these " zones " is, however, purely relative, and depends upon the position of what we may call the " dramatic centre of the stage." In Fig. 5, the dramatic centre of the stage may be said to be somewhere within the figure formed by ABEF. That is to say, the drama of the play is being carried by the bulk of the characters, whose positions are within the space represented by that figure. Consequently X, who is outside that space, does not appear as part of the scene. But if as in Fig. 7 we move D some distance up-stage and E some distance up-stage and to the right, we are shifting the dramatic centre of the stage to somewhere within the figure ABDXEF, as well as suggesting the triangle AXF, of which X is the apex and therefore in the dominant position. By doing this we have made X important, in spite of his being so far towards the back of the stage. Note how characters A, B, D and F, E all tend to lead the eye

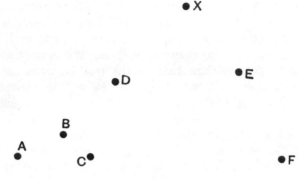

FIG. 7.

onward and upward towards X, thereby concentrating attention upon him; while in Fig. 6 they seemed to lead nowhere in particular.

Obviously it is not always essential for actual characters to form the apices of these imaginary triangles. For instance, in Fig. 8—

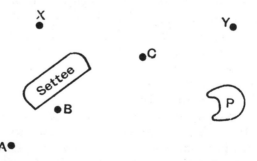

FIG. 8.

it is not X or Y who has the dominating position, but

C, who forms the apex of the triangle made by A, C, and the chair P.

It must be clearly understood that this perception and creation of triangles must not be taken too literally. The audience must never be conscious of a geometric grouping and the producer should never consciously formulate such grouping. Indeed, the triangles in any case are purely approximate, since the greatest crime that a producer may commit in the arrangement of his characters is to place them in anything approaching a straight line. Thus in Fig. 7 the characters A, B, D and X could never be in exactly the positions shown : if they were, X would be able to see D but not B or A, and D would be able to see B, but not A, C would be masking both B and D from various parts of the auditorium, and so on. We have shown certain principles of stage grouping by the use of triangles : but beyond that, triangles have no further function.

These principles must be modified by a number of other considerations. For instance, it is important that no character should hide or " mask " any other character from any part of the audience—unless the character masked is one of no great dramatic importance at that particular moment. It is important, too, that all characters should stand so as to be able to see those whom they are supposed to be addressing. Producers should also consider that what is true in the horizontal plane will also be true in the vertical plane, in which imaginary triangles could also be formed. A character who is standing, for instance, is more dominant than one who is sitting, even though the sitting character may be farther up-stage than is the former. In all cases where common sense would seem to combat any theory of grouping, the producer will be wise to let the theory go overboard, otherwise his effect will seem forced and stilted.

So far we have dealt with grouping which achieves its purpose by doing the expected. The eye is gently led towards the expected dominant position, and there it finds the dominant character—on the spot, as if by arrangement (which is only too true). But there can be virtue in doing the very reverse and thus achieving emphasis by sheer contrast. For though the eye of the audience undoubtedly has this tendency to wander and to seek a focal point, *yet it will not do so if the character whom it is watching has lines and action of sufficient importance to fix its constant attention.*

Value of the Unexpected Therefore at any big dramatic moment in a performance it will often be of value deliberately to forget all the principles of geometric grouping, and to place the dominant character in the place where he is least expected, or where normally he would be of least importance. For instance in Fig. 9,

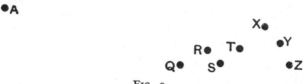

FIG. 9.

A stands out emphatically upon the stage by very reason of his isolation from the other characters, QRSTXYZ. In spite of the fact that this group forms the dramatic centre of the stage, A remains the important figure, and he will continue to be important wherever he goes, provided he keeps his distance. But the moment he becomes near enough to the group to become identified with it, his importance vanishes. For this reason a producer wishing to prepare an effective entrance for an important character will move the bulk of his other characters to a part of the stage remote from that point at which the entrance is to be made. In doing this he isolates his entering character from the dramatic centre of the stage, and emphasizes the entrance by forcibly shifting the attention of the audience towards an unexpected direction. The resulting dramatic effect is almost that of a shock—comparable to a sudden vocal contrast or a pistol shot. A similar effect is obtained by making a character, who for the moment has nothing to say, move up-stage and turn his back upon the audience. When a dramatic moment occurs which concerns this character, he may turn and speak : his sudden return to the scene at this point will emphasize the lines he has to say.

Décor. An audience should be stimulated by the *décor* of a performance, and thus kept in a suitably receptive state, in the same way that they should be stimulated by contrasts of movement, grouping and variety of speech.

The term *décor* includes the entire pictorial aspect of a performance—setting, lighting, arrangement of the furniture and general decoration. Its functions are three—stimulative, interpretative, and decorative.

In this chapter we are only concerned with its stimulative function. For this purpose the important quality in the *décor* is that it should have some sort of form which is refreshing and unexpected, without being in any way startling or distracting. This form is of course determined by the shape of the actual setting, in which at the present time (particularly with interior settings) far too little imagination is usually shown in the theatre. The majority of plays seem to take place in a setting like this :

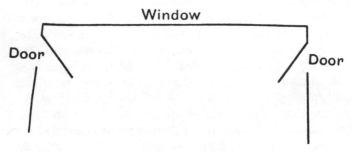

FIG. 10.

Now this may, or may not, convey the idea to some people of the interior of a room. But its most noticeable feature is that it is completely lacking in any special quality. There is nothing about it to command the attention. As with the rectangle in Fig. 1 the eye wanders restlessly around its sides without focusing upon anything particular. As a background to a three-act play it is difficult to imagine anything duller. In order to avoid this monotony nothing is simpler than to break the straight sides of the walls, thus :

FIG. 11.

Such ground plans as these would provide settings

with just that difference from the ordinary which is part of the attraction of the theatre. As can be seen, there is practically no limit to the variations which are possible, for the smallest alteration of feature will often be enough to alter the entire balance of the setting.

Very often a play will be so written that some architectural feature in the setting will assume a definite dramatic significance. The entrance of a leading character at a dramatic moment may invest the door at which he enters with a very particular importance, in which case it will be most valuable to emphasize that door in the making of the scene. Now the setting in Fig. 10, by its very nature, makes it impossible to emphasize any particular feature ; but by evolving a scene on the same principles as those employed in emphatic grouping it is easy to make any part of the scene as dominant as one wishes.

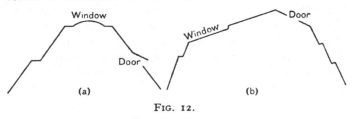

FIG. 12.

In Fig. 12 (a) it is the window which is emphasized ; in (b) it is the door. In each case the eye is led to rest upon the important features by the general trend of the side walls.

The need for this variety in the setting does not, of course, mean that the square setting should *never* be used. There are numberless plays written of which the *locale* is such that it does not permit of any great departure from the conventional : in these cases it is often part of the dramatic intention of the play that the setting should suggest monotony. But it is possible to suggest monotony without being dreary. For instance, in Fig. 13—

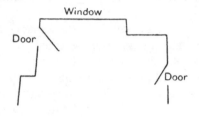

FIG. 13.

the squareness of the room is suggested, yet the straight lines are broken up and complete monotony consequently avoided.

Another virtue of this method is that it gives a suggestion of thickness to the walls. The wide expanse of plane surface in Fig. 10 can so easily convey an impression of wafer-like instability, while the many angles in the other ground plans, when viewed from the auditorium, will suggest a far greater degree of solidity.

With exterior scenes the danger of monotony is smaller : the producer-designer has greater freedom of choice. Also he can make greater use here of the third dimension by a judicious use of the rostrum or platform. The Rostrum can be a boon to any producer, for in addition to assisting him in the avoidance of masking, he can by varying the height of different portions of the stage obtain a completely new set of emphatic values. The moment a character is placed upon a rostrum he becomes a dominant feature of the scene, no matter

Use of the Rostrum

where that rostrum may be placed : therefore variety in the vertical plane may be used together with variety in the horizontal plane.

The two may act as complementaries or in opposition. King Lear, raised high upon his dais, towers above his subjects and ruthlessly condemns the faithful Kent to banishment : here is dramatic domination in the vertical plane. But when Regan and Goneril speak, they speak from the up-stage position to Lear who, though on a rostrum, is yet in the subordinate down stage position : here is dramatic domination in the horizontal plane. The two sets of values are useful in showing the opposing aspects of Lear's position in his kingdom. If Lear were placed in the dominant up-stage part of the scene, the two values would support each other : Lear's dignity and strength would be increased, and the two sisters would never be able fully to express their true natures.

Another quality of the rostrum is that the people upon it, by reason of their difference in physical plane, can be made to appear remote and separate from all action carried on upon the normal level. On a small stage this is particularly valuable, for the producer is often faced with the problem of making effective a scene in which two or three of the characters have lines which are ostensibly out of hearing of the rest of the people of the play. The placing of those characters on a rostrum will effectively separate them in spirit, if not in fact ; for this makes it easy for the audience to accept the convention that the two groups cannot overhear each other.

To the arrangement of furniture upon the stage the same principles apply as those that affect grouping : the avoidance of arrangements in line, of any conscious suggestion of a geometrical figure, of any arrangement which creates a dreary effect (such as a large table placed *exactly* in the centre of a room), and a general regard for the freedom and convenience of the actors are the chief considerations. The space around entrances and exits should be left clear enough to allow characters to come on and off cleanly. There should always be plenty of room for movement around the various pieces, and easy access should be obtainable to all parts of the stage. The furniture should not be too near the footlights, as this will prevent intimate scenes from being played in close enough contact with the audience.

The lighting of the scene will depend upon the nature of the play ; here it need only be said that lighting should also play its part in obtaining variety. The stage should never be bathed in a profusion of even " flat " light. This may take all character out of the faces of the actors, and by removing any sense of mystery completely spoil the atmosphere of a play. Light should be used in varying tones and values, to emphasize some parts of the stage more than others, so that in addition to the values obtained by the character's position on the vertical or horizontal plane, further degrees of emphasis may result from the degree of illumination upon him.

VI. INTERPRETATION IN PRODUCTION

IT is a truism that all plays are written in some sort of convention. Whether they be naturalistic, poetic, or melodramatic, they all demand that the audience shall accept them as convincing on certain terms, and the convention depends upon the nature of those terms.

Conventions in Play-writing

A realistic play such as " Journey's End," for instance, asks the audience to regard, from its own world of plush seats and rococo decoration, another world of mud and war, whose inhabitants are enacting the drama of their own lives, oblivious to any other plane of existence. In spite of the fact that the setting of this play demands a dug-out three times the size of the genuine article ; that its fourth wall has been removed for the audience's inspection ; and that the side walls of earth and pit props merge so incongruously with the gilded cherubs of the stage boxes—in spite of these and a dozen other negations of reality, yet will the audience accept the convention that " the play is real " provided certain rules are rigidly maintained. For example, the audience, having made the initial pretence that it is not in a theatre at all but is regarding " real life," must not be asked to pretend any more. Everything that happens behind the proscenium arch must carry the conviction of reality : uniforms must be accurate, machine-guns must sound like machine-guns, soldiers must behave as soldiers would, and so on. This is the *naturalistic* convention.

Its characters demand acceptance as recognizable portraits of human beings as we know them : its life is the life of our world depicted upon the stage.

Shakespeare wrote in a different convention. He did not seek to evade the limitations of the playhouse. He asked his audiences not to forget the fact that they were in a theatre but to accept it, and, while accepting it, to listen to his fairy-tales. His actors, playing Hamlet or King Lear, did not say in effect, " I am Hamlet " or " I am King Lear " : they said " I, with my talent, and the author, with his crafts-manship and his poetry, will now help you to imagine Hamlet and King Lear." Consequently there was no dividing-line between audience and player : the pro-scenium was unnecessary, and so were the trappings of realistic make-believe that went with it ; accurate representation of costume and scene had no place. This we may call the purely *theatrical* convention.

These two conventions stand at opposite ends of the scale, the first with its material appeal to verisimilitude, the second with its appeal entirely to the imagination. Between them lie many more : the farcical convention, in which ordinary people are involved in fantastic happenings ; the melodramatic convention which, soaring above the clouds of fancy, yet clings to a basis of the most complete realism—and so on.

The convention chosen by the playwright depends upon what he most wishes to express, and in choosing that convention which assists him most, he sacrifices what he considers the inessentials. Shakespeare in his convention sacrificed realism, and by excluding the externals of life more easily exposed its inner truths. To the realistic writer it is often those very super-ficial aspects with which he is most concerned ; therefore to him the inner significances do not matter.

The producer's business, when faced for the first time with his material, is to discover the particular convention in which it is written. And, having discovered it, it is his business to ensure that the quality of the performance shall be consistent with it, and that nothing in the manner of an actor's speaking or moving, and no element in the grouping and *décor* shall be such as to break it. Having determined the convention of the play and consequently his own general method in dealing with it, he can then pass on to consideration of the characters. And he will find that characters, like plays, are also written within the limits of a convention ; that the author has deliberately stressed certain facets of character at the expense of certain others, in order to create a particular, definite picture, which the actor may embellish, but must not distort.

Now the convention of a play may be compared to the key of a piece of music. In altering the key of a tune, each note may be a tone higher or lower, but the notes remain the same in relation to each other. The tune has not been changed, though by being put in a different key its character has been subtly altered. In the same way, a play may be *written* in one convention, but *played* in another.

Such transposition of the convention the producer may be frequently called upon to make, particularly in the case of plays of another period, of which the convention has so far gone out of fashion as to be out of tune with modern sympathies. The case for transposition is well exemplified in Oscar Wilde's " The Importance of Being Earnest." The stilted mannerisms of language which this author employed were regarded as the correct *stage method* of depicting fashionable witty conversation. The fact that men and women never spoke like that in the nineties or at any other time did not matter ; it was a convention that they did, and therefore Wilde wrote his play within that convention. But if that same convention is employed in its production to-day the modern audience will find the play completely unreal and absurd. It no longer accepts the convention that Wilde's long and completely uncolloquial speeches are true to life, and therefore the spectacle of modern actors reciting them in front of a perfectly naturalistic background seems ridiculous. Thus the modern producer changes the key. Instead of making his actors play sincerely and " straight," he fantasticates them, emphasizes, with just a touch of burlesque, the polished complexities of their speech, and puts them in front of flimsy highly-decorated backgrounds of screens or curtains. Instead of having put new wine into an old bottle he has, so to speak, made a new bottle of a different shape out of the material of the old. In the new convention the play becomes alive again : the values have been altered—nothing in the piece can now be taken seriously—but they remain the same in their relation to each other. The result is that the entire piece of theatre—play, actors and scenery—still forms a consistent whole.

It is this quality of *consistency* which the producer must, at all costs, attain. To take a play out of the convention for which it was intended and to produce it in a convention of one's own may or may not be artistically defensible ; it depends on so **Importance of** many factors, such as the period of **Consistency** the play, the suitability or otherwise of the convention for the author's purpose (the author must usually be given credit for knowing best what he is trying to say)—and in any case the justification can only be by the result. But not to be definite and consistent within whatever convention one may choose—that is almost the greatest crime one may commit in the theatre. There is, for instance, every justification for departing from Shakespeare's convention, since nowadays the public finds it almost impossible to accept. But there is no justification for not realizing that Shakespeare wrote his descriptive passages of superb poetry in order to compensate for his lack of scenery, and that therefore his most vivid descriptions—the storm scene in " King Lear," for instance—almost make scenery unnecessary. The producer—only too common—who swamps his " Lear " with petty exhibitions of rain, thunder, lightning and blasted heath, is thoroughly inconsistent since he is applying a realistic background to what can never by its very poetic nature be anything but an un-realistic scene. Worse than that, he is committing the mistake of giving his audience two simultaneous effects at the same time. Who can appreciate the beauty of

> Blow, winds, and crack your cheeks ! rage ! blow !
> You cataracts and hurricanoes, spout
> Till you have drenched the steeples, drown'd the
>   cocks !
> You sulphurous and thought-executing fires,
> Vaunt couriers to oak-cleaving thunderbolts,
> Singe my white head !

if he is distracted by the billowing of scenery and the clatter of the rain-box in the wings ? The producer of " Lear " is free to choose what convention he likes with the obvious exception that absolute realism is impossible without inconsistency.

It would seem therefore that even more important

than a producer's understanding of the play's convention is his understanding and consciousness of his
own convention : whatever he does, he
Convention in Production must consciously produce his material in
such a way that it acquires, in presenta-
tion, a consistent " personality."

His method of working will be influenced most
powerfully—by the convention he chooses to employ
—according to whether that convention leans most
towards the naturalistic or towards the theatrical.
For, although the conventions are many, they all tend
to fall into one or the other of these two main groups :
either an audience is asked to believe in " reality "
in the theatre, or it is asked to believe in " make-
believe." These two divisions will form a convenient
basis from which to examine interpretation in terms
of dialogue, of movement, of individual characterization, and finally of *décor*.

1. Dialogue.

The fundamental difference between the naturalistic
mood or convention and the theatrical mood, in so far
as it affects the actor and producer, is as follows :
characters in the theatrical mood display, to a greater
or lesser degree, their emotions unfettered and undis-
guised, and their conduct need not be limited within
the confines of probability, nor of the restraint imposed
by conventional social behaviour. On the other hand,
characters in the naturalistic mood usually tend to dis-
guise and control their emotions, and their conduct on
the surface is strictly limited by the prevailing code of
social manners.

Consequently the drama of the theatrical convention is frequently carried upon the surface of the
dialogue, while that of the naturalistic convention

is often implied beneath the lines. The prevailing characteristic of the former is freedom, that of the latter, restraint. The former will support broad effects and big contrasts, the latter will demand contrasts of the greatest subtlety. In the theatrical key we may play every note from the highest to the lowest : in the naturalistic key we may only play half the notes, and those with the soft pedal ; but, as if in compensation, our touch must be the more delicate.

The following scene from " Journey's End " is a perfect example of the naturalistic method :

RALEIGH. We're having something special for dinner, aren't we ?

OSBOURNE. How did you know ? It's supposed to be a secret.

RALEIGH. Mason dropped a hint.

OSBOURNE. Well, we've had a fresh chicken sent up from Noyelle Farm.

RALEIGH. I say !

OSBOURNE. And a most awful luxury—two bottles of champagne and half a dozen cigars ! One each and one spare one in case one explodes.

RALEIGH. I've never smoked a cigar.

OSBOURNE. It's bound to make you sick.

(RALEIGH *notices* OSBOURNE'S *ring on the table ; he picks it up*.)

RALEIGH. I say, here's your ring.

OSBOURNE. Yes. I'm—I'm leaving it here. I don't want the risk of losing it.

RALEIGH. Oh !

(*There is silence. He puts the ring slowly down.*)

OSBOURNE (*rising*). Well, I think perhaps we ought to get ready.

RALEIGH. Yes. Righto. (*He also rises.*)

OSBOURNE. I'm not going to wear a belt—just my revolver with the lanyard round my neck.

RALEIGH. I see.

(*He puts his lanyard round his neck and grips his revolver.*)

I feel better with this in my hand, don't you ?

OSBOURNE. Yes. Something to hold. Loaded all right ?

RALEIGH. Yes.

As so often happens in real life, nothing is *said* in this scene which exceeds the bounds of ordinary conversation. The words themselves carry no drama at all. When the climax is reached and Raleigh sees the ring, all that happens is :

OSBOURNE. Yes. I'm—I'm leaving it here. I don't want the risk of losing it.

RALEIGH. Oh !

The casual commonplace " Yes " and the pause after it together say all that need be said : in effect—" Yes. I'm taking it off because I know that I am practically certain to be killed, and I should like my wife to have it after I am dead." Each of the other commonplace lines seems similarly, though in a lesser degree, to cloak emotions which, though disguised, are none the less deep and poignant. There is no difficulty here in finding and making the proper dramatic contrasts. The difficulty lies in making them in such a way that the naturalistic convention is not broken. *For, so often, when we say that an actor over-acts or that a play becomes theatrical (meaning " false ") at a certain point, we mean that the actor or the play has slipped out of the convention which it appeared we were intended to accept.* What may be brilliant acting in one convention will be a hopeless outflow of false emphases in another.

The convention of " Journey's End " demands such restraint in the use of language and of expression as amounts almost to clumsiness—a clumsiness which does not matter, because the drama is conveyed not by the language but by its implications. Yet in pointing these implications to the audience the same restraint must be employed if the convention is to be preserved intact. The contrasts must be of the most delicate kind ; the tonal changes must be scarcely perceptible, though definite ; the dramatic pauses must not be too long, too pointed, yet they must be marked, for it is essential that they be not lost. For instance, in Osbourne's line about the ring :

Yes . . . . . . I'm leaving it here.

the pause after the " Yes " must be just long enough to do its work—to tell the audience what Osbourne is feeling and what Raleigh is feeling—but it must not be one second longer than that : the slightest over-emphasis will seem to be over-acting, and will spoil what is one of the most impressive moments of the play

The character of dialogue may be expressed even more by its *tempo*, perhaps, than by the vocal con-

Tempo   trasts of its delivery. The *tempo* of naturalistic dialogue must have infinite variety. Where words themselves say so little, a pause will convey a very great deal.

HE. Are you happy here ?
SHE. Yes.

According to the length of time she allows to elapse before she makes her answer that " Yes " can be made to mean : (1) A most emphatic affirmative. (Spoken quickly and definitely on the cue.) (2) An

apparent affirmative defiantly cloaking the very reverse. (Spoken with very extreme quickness on the
cue.) (3) Uncertainty. (A short pause, for thought,
before answering.) (4) An implied, yet definite nega-
tive. (Spoken after a long pause.) Thus another
function of the dramatic pause is to convey varying
degrees of thought : the longer the pause before a
word or a statement the greater the depth of thought
behind it.

The theatrical convention, represented here by the
excerpt from " Othello " and the Harker-Mason dialogue, on page 41, demands a different method. The
Harker-Mason dialogue is frankly melodramatic. The
producer here may give the words the uttermost
emphasis that they are capable of sustaining, *consistent
with their value*. Here are no hidden subtleties : the
words mean what they say and no more, and the
drama is carried by them on the surface. Hence the
treatment they demand is bolder. Instead of the
multitudinous, yet tiny, contrasts that give colour to
naturalistic dialogue, the effects will be broad and
sweeping. Yet even melodrama is tinctured with
realism ; we like to believe that its events, though
improbable, may yet sometimes occur in life. So
that, even with melodrama, the full scale of dramatic
expression may not be used ; for it is often concerned
with people like ourselves, and it is not considered
proper for civilized social beings to expose their
emotions too fully.

Complete freedom is only achieved with poetic drama
at its best. Shakespeare did not write about people
as such. They were magnificent, vivid, alive creatures,
but they were not really people. " Othello " is not just
a story of an innocent wife murdered by an insanely
jealous husband : the Moor is the complete expression

of the *idea* of jealousy, and Desdemona transcends mere humanity to become the personification of trusting innocence. With Shakespeare the producer is free. He can treat his dialogue as a conductor treats music, and explore every nuance of volume, tone and *tempo*, without having continually to pander to " probability " and " verisimilitude."

2. Movement.

The types of movement most frequently employed in a performance will depend upon the convention in which it is produced. In so far as it is ever safe to generalize about methods in the theatre it may be said that :

The theatrical convention will permit of all kinds of movement.

The naturalistic convention will confine the producer in most cases to the use of unconscious movement only.

This is only consistent with what we have already determined, for while the theatrical convention provides almost infinite freedom of treatment, the naturalistic convention demands that no manifestation should occur in the theatre which could not be matched with a similar and common manifestation in life.

CONSCIOUS MOVEMENT. Now in life our movements are rarely conscious movements, except in those cases where they are dictated by purely practical considerations. We may move consciously to open a window, but we very rarely find ourselves moving in the manner of Harker or Mason [1] : if we saw anybody doing so we might be struck by the artificiality of his action ; we would say he was theatrical. Normally our natural

[1] See page 41.

movements would seem to have no particular meaning or purpose. But if we ever find ourselves in circumstances in the least dramatic, our movements do become in some degree conscious. If we are angry with a person we might move towards him as we display our anger : in fear of him, we might shrink away.

Now, as dialogue becomes more theatrical, more " dramatic," its drama approaches the surface. Therefore we may say that

> In the naturalistic convention conscious movement other than that with a practical purpose is only permissible when the drama is upon the surface of the lines.

As we have already seen, such movement can have great dramatic value, and it is to some extent of interpretative significance. It is in Harker's character as a strong man to move as he does, and in Mason's as a weak one to back, frightened, away. But beyond conveying such broad effects as courage, dominance or fear, the conscious movement is limited in its power to suggest character since the opportunities for using it are few and are determined by the nature of the scene. Neither Harker nor Mason could have moved in this manner had their relative positions been different : the inspiration for their movements came not from within themselves but from their situation.

Unconscious movement, on the other hand, may be indicative of character, of mental state and of the very mood of a play. For it is part of a character's own personality, as peculiar to him as his own face, and therefore as capable of expressing his thoughts and emotions as the words he speaks and the actions he performs. It can suggest so many things that it is worthy of some analysis.

Let us imagine a character holding forth among his friends upon some pet theory of his own. He wishes to put forward a point of view in which he passionately believes, and as he warms to his subject, feeling his way from argument to argument, making a point here and a point there, he begins to parade, quite unconsciously, up and down his hearthrug. Now, why does he walk up and down ? The movement, though natural, is perfectly meaningless. Yet he does this nervous *unnecessary* act because, like smoking, it probably helps him to array his thoughts in suitable formation. It is a weakness : if he had complete control of himself he would undoubtedly keep still. But while all his strength is occupied in controlling his thought, he has none left with which to control his body. Yet the moment he sees his way ahead along the road of his argument he will once more stand still ; for in ceasing his process of concentrated thought, and simply allowing the results of that process to flow in a fluent stream, his brain is sufficiently relieved to control his nervous energy.

Now we can imagine a man, who in spite of this groping process in his mind, may yet have sufficient control to keep perfectly still : to him we would assign the virtues of poise and strength.

We may therefore tabulate the allied attributes of unconscious movement, and of its opposite, repose.

UNCONSCIOUS MOVEMENT. This may denote (1) a certain lack of control, due (2) to a process of more or less concentrated *unresolved* thought. If we elaborate from (1) we may say that lack of control suggests a dissipation of energy, a scattering of forces, weakness, irresolution, any situation where the character is not master of himself, lack of dignity and emotion which is not dominated by the mind. Elaborating from

(2) we get any uncertain mental state, introspection, preoccupation, etc.

REPOSE. This, conversely, may suggest complete control, strength, certitude, poise, any emotion which the mind has been able to dominate, and any process of thought which has been resolved and completed.

The nature of the dialogue will tell us whether or not it permits of movement. In Hamlet's " To be, or not to be," soliloquy we have the expression of a process of thought, groping, indeterminate and completely unpractical. Hamlet is living in the far-off reaches of his mind : his body is forgotten. Consequently suitable unconscious movements in the right place will help to convey his character as well as providing contrasts by breaking up what is a very long speech. On the other hand, Polonius' speech to Laertes on his departure for England is of a very different kind, for here the speaker is of some authority. Polonius may be a fool and a bore, but he possesses a certain dignity ; his speech is eminently practical and is that of a man communicating certain precepts, *of which he is sure*, to ᴗomeone younger and of less experience than himself. For Polonius to move here would be to rob him of any authority at all. Again, the instructions of the Colonel in " Journey's End " would be spoken from a fixed position, for the man has poise and stɪength : he is not thinking, but is communicating to others the results of his thought. On the other hand, we may say of Ford in Act IV, Scene 2, of the " Merry Wives of Windsor " that he is not thinking, either : yet must he stand still while he is raging about the supposed presence of Falstaff in his house ? The answer is, of course, that he may stamp about and move as much as he likes, for he is so maddened with jealousy that this emotion has long ago succeeded in dominating his mind : he is in no way under control, and there is scarcely a limit to the amount of storming up and down that he may do. Timon of Athens, in Act IV, Scene 1, of the play, though his emotions are to be seriously regarded, is in precisely the same position : he is pouring out a torrent of feeling, uncontrolled, and without a trace of thought behind it : consequently, he too may move at those points where it will seem natural for him to do so.

The direction in which a movement is made is a matter of some importance. Let us refer again to the two movements in the Harker-Mason dialogue on page 41. The first—that of Harker *towards* Mason— has an effect apart from its effect on Mason and its reflection of Harker's character. It has an effect of increasing the suspense and tightening the dramatic tension, for it is pregnant with all sorts of dramatic possibilities which are none the less effective because they do not eventuate. In performance an audience would be in a state of mild, excited suspense, as they wondered just exactly why Harker was moving towards Mason and just exactly what he was proposing to do. The second movement has precisely the opposite effect : it relaxes the suspense and loosens the tension ; to the audience it would be the signal that they could breathe again.

Since these are conscious dramatic movements the qualities of suspense and relief are present to a very great degree. It is, however, to some extent true of all movements to say that those of one character or characters towards another or others create a general, if vague, atmosphere of heightened suspense. And the converse is also true, that a general atmosphere of relief and loosening of tension is caused by a movement of characters outwards and away from each other.

3. Individual Characterization.

The characterization of a part is largely a question for the actor himself ; its problems have been excellently dealt with in numerous books on the art of Acting, which go into the matter in considerable detail.

The producer's duty is to ensure that the actor has a correct idea of the interpretation of the part, that his interpretation keeps within the bounds of the convention of the part and of the play, and that his performance is such that, while exploiting to the full the part's potentialities yet does not hinder the equally full exploitation of all the other parts in the play.

That the producer and the actor should agree as to the interpretation of a part is, not unnaturally, of paramount importance ; particularly as it is always the actor, once the curtain has gone up on the first performance, who has the last word in any controversy. A good actor should be given credit for having an intelligent view of the character he is trying to express : none the less, if the producer is to succeed in keeping his convention consistent and creating a coherent and shapely piece of Theatre his ruling on such matters should be final.

The producer must have a very definite picture in his mind of the nature and personality of every character in the play. Otherwise he may find himself at a loss over many problems of interpretation where the slightest variation of an inflexion may completely alter the sense. The following oft-quoted passage from " Macbeth," where Lady Macbeth is urging her husband to proceed with the murder of Duncan, is an excellent example of the way a subtle change of intonation may alter values :

LADY MACBETH.   . . . I have given suck and know
                  How tender 'tis to love the babe that
                    milks me :
                  I would, while it was smiling in my face,
                  Have pluck'd my nipple from his boneless gums,
                  And dash'd the brains out, had I so sworn as you
                  Have done to this.
MACBETH.   If we should fail——
LADY MACBETH.   We fail !
                  But screw your courage to the sticking-place,
                  And we'll not fail.

How should the words " we fail " be spoken ? Modern editors of Shakespeare append the exclamation mark, which might suggest arrogance, scorn, or amazement, according to the inflexion. When Mrs. Siddons played the part it was reputed that she spoke the words as if they were followed by a full stop, and in a low, definite fatalistic tone suggesting : " If we fail, why, then we just fail, that's all." On the other hand the Folio of 1623 prints a question mark after the words, which definitely demands an upward inflexion and suggests incredulous astonishment.

There are doubtless many other readings, and the choice of any particular one must be determined by whether or not it is consistent with the rest of the character. For different actresses in different productions any one of these readings may or may not be correct : for any particular actress in any one production *only one is right*—and that the one which accords with her method throughout the other acts of the play.

It is this consistency which the producer, by virtue of his position outside the performance, must always strive to maintain, and he can only maintain it by having formed beforehand in his own mind a complete picture of *his* Lady Macbeth and how she would behave, not only in these circumstances but in others of his own imagining.

This means that the producer must have an intimate knowledge of his characters, and that in judging how various portions of dialogue should be spoken he will constantly look ahead, and examine not only the nature of the speeches as they appear, but also the nature of the speeches which follow them. Only by doing this can he keep his characters within their proper conventions, and express convincingly the emotional and mental transitions through which they pass.

An example of the importance of this occurs in Act I, Scene 2, of " Hamlet," where Hamlet, after a period of restrained and fairly normal behaviour in the presence of the King and Queen, bursts immediately upon their exit into the speech beginning :

O, that this too too solid flesh would melt !

This soliloquy is an outburst of the most violent nature. Yet the lines which have led up to it are quiet enough, and there has been no indication in them of any particular emotional stress. If, however, these lines are spoken as superficially it might appear they should be spoken—that is, merely softly and in a controlled manner—the contrast provided by Hamlet's subsequent flow of emotion will be too great, too sudden, to seem appropriate. And, unless the audience can *see* this emotion welling up within Hamlet *before* the exit of the King and Queen, they will find the later transition to it artificial—and the whole soliloquy will seem false and exaggerated. Therefore the actor playing Hamlet must show the existence of this submerged emotion *in the first part of the scene*, before he can, convincingly, allow it to burst forth in the second part. He will show this to the audience with his eyes, his facial expression, and perhaps the slightest tremor in his voice, while at the same time giving to the rest of the characters an exhibition of apparent, superficial restraint.

From this it will be seen how important it is to keep characters " alive " and identified with their parts, even when they have nothing to say at all. When a character is without lines for three or four minutes the producer must see that he continues during this period silently to *act* ; so that, when his turn comes, he will be able to slip smoothly into the emotional key which the other characters have given to the scene. By such silent acting it is not, of course, meant that the speechless performer should do anything violent in the way of gesture or movement. This would of necessity be a distraction from the effect of the speaking characters. All that is necessary is the use of appropriate facial expression—and an appearance of intelligent interest in what is happening upon the stage. This applies to *all* characters who are before the footlights, but have, for the moment, nothing to say.

A small gesture, a lifting of the eyebrow, or turning of the head, or an appropriate piece of business
Stage Business at the right moment will often characterize more vividly than words : it is a fault of many plays—so often written by people with no practical knowledge of the theatre — that they try to convey too much by dialogue. The

D

producer or actor who can substitute, for the words which the audience expects, a gesture which will convey the meaning just as well, is contributing a variety and freshness to the performance which is invaluable.

But stage business must never appear to be forced ; and for that reason it is wise not to insist upon a particular effect unless the actor is capable of " feeling " it. A feeling for business is so much a personal matter for the actor, and so much a matter of intuition, that he may often feel uncomfortable when the suggestion comes from someone else. And if he is uncomfortable he will not do his business well. It was said that Irving used to do a remarkable piece of business in his performance of " King Lear." Upon the line :

Be your tears wet ? Yes, faith. I pray, weep not :

he put his hand to Cordelia's wet cheek and slowly bringing it to his lips, tasted the tears upon it. No doubt, this was a most poignant moment in his performance : certainly it must have conveyed to the full the old king's reduction to a madness infinitely pathetic in its childishness. But to impose such business upon an actor to whom it had not intuitively occurred might be extremely dangerous, for unless it were done with the utmost delicacy and spontaneity, the result might be a ludicrous over-weighting of the part.

One mistake in business may easily cause a performance to fall completely out of its proper convention. Particularly is this true of business which has been inserted merely for the sake of getting a cheap laugh. Unfortunately " clever " business is often the hallmark of the " clever " producer ; and the temptation to show how inventive one is, by burdening a play with too much business, is a temptation to be resisted.

The producer will have, however, more frequently to restrain the actor than himself. Often an actor may wish to make a gesture or a piece of business which may appear to him to be natural, but which, viewed in relation to the performance as a whole, might be superfluous and out of place. Business and gesture are subject to the ordinary principles of stage movement : however natural they may appear to the actor, they must be ruthlessly cut out if they seem likely to distract attention from more important things.

4. Décor and Grouping.

Proper grouping in a performance will often possess great dramatic value. The entire significance of a scene may be crystallized and retained in the audience's mind, by the visual relationships of its characters, long after the words those characters have spoken may have been forgotten. Stark Young[1] has expressed this well :

" In the . . . production of ' Hamlet ' . . . the scene where Hamlet comes upon the King at prayer was acted with the King on his knees near the front of the stage, his hands lifted to heaven. Behind him stood Hamlet with his drawn sword in his hand. The two figures, one behind the other, the lifted hands, the sword pointing, expressed for the eye the exact pattern of the scene's idea, the precise theme of relationships. Visually, at least, the essential of that scene had been achieved, and had been freed of every characteristic not its own."

In the main, sensible interpretative grouping consists merely of the logical application of the various principles of grouping which we have already dis-

[1] *Theatre Practice*, by Stark Young. Charles Scribner's Sons. 1926.

cussed. That is, each character should reflect, in each part of the play, his dramatic relation to his fellows by the linear relation that he takes up in regard to them. Thus, dominating characters will assume the dominating positions ; the various entrances and exits will be emphasized according to their relative importance ; intimate scenes will be played close to the footlights and near the audience, and so on. The qualities which will be of most service to the producer will once more be those of common sense and a natural instinct for dramatic propriety.

The *décor* presents a more difficult problem in that it must be complementary to a play and help to express its atmosphere, while at the same time its design is so often in the hands of some outside scenic expert. It cannot be stated too often that the scenic side of the theatre is just as much the producer's business as rehearsing the actors in the way they should go. The producer is responsible for the setting even if he has not executed it ; it is therefore wise for him to be responsible for his own mistakes instead of those of other people.

The objection to the scenic artist rests on very solid grounds which are implied in his very title. The scenic painter considers himself an artist, and with the best of good intentions he will not be able to resist the temptation to " put a bit of himself " into the work he has to do, and to leave the mark of his own personality upon it. Now the creator of scenery is not an artist in the sense that a sculptor or a musician is an artist. For the sculptor, when he has finished his work, has created something which is complete in itself, while the scene designer, if he has done his work properly, has only created what must be a part—and a subservient part—of the whole : he has supplied the pictorial factor in a piece of theatre, and that factor only does its work in conjunction with all the other factors. Consequently the designer must subjugate his own interests to the interests of the whole : he must not, however unwittingly, express *himself* ; he must express *the play*. As it is the producer's duty to see that this is done, so is it wise for him to do it himself. A producer who cannot create his own scenery is like a conductor who will condescend to conduct the strings and the wood-wind but cannot undertake to control the antics of the brass.

The type of setting will depend upon the convention of the play, and will therefore tend either towards the naturalistic or the theatrical.

The naturalistic convention will not demand realism, but a *suggestion* of realism. Elaborate and meticulous realism will invariably defeat its own object, for it will always challenge the audience to compare it with real life. The more remarkable the deception the more conscious will the audience be that it *is a deception*, and the more will they occupy their minds with thinking of the scenery instead of the play. An example of this was the recent London production of " Cavalcade," at which the audience marvelled far more over a reconstruction of Victoria Station, and the presence on the stage of a real London omnibus, than they ever did over the writing or the acting. This was putting the cart before the horse with a vengeance.

The secret of good naturalistic scenery is that it should be simple, that it should be solid and firm, that it should be pleasant to look upon yet not obtrusive, and that as well as defining without doubt the *locale* of the play it should convey an atmosphere in keeping with the play's own special quality.

The simplicity of a good setting consists in stressing the essentials of form and line, and giving a suggestion of the reality from which those essentials are taken ; then leaving the rest to the imagination of the audience. A simplified Gothic arch in a neutral-coloured wall will suggest a church far better than an elaborate attempt to depict each stone and each pane of glass. An eighteenth-century drawing-room may be perfectly conveyed by the furniture of the period, a background with windows of the correct proportions and a simplified Adam dado around the walls. Even with the most realistic plays it is remarkable how much may be left to the imagination, for the audience will accept the greatest degree of simplification, provided the essentials are there ; but it will not stand for shaking scenery and flapping canvas. For this reason it is wise to avoid doors wherever possible. Doors which open and shut have a most unsettling effect on the surrounding walls, even in the best regulated theatres ; and they are not often really necessary, unless demanded by some particular piece of business in the plot of the play.

The colour of the setting depends upon the play, to which it must be sympathetic. It is an old convention that for a comedy one must have a light setting, while for a tragic play a dark background is necessary. This is only partly true. Certainly, it is hard to " put over " comedy in front of a dark background ; but it is equally hard to put over a tragedy with scenery that may be in the least depressing. The less brightness there may be in a play, the more important is it that the scenery, while consistent with the play's atmosphere, should be cheerful—if possible.

In the theatrical convention the producer is far freer in his opportunities, for he can escape from the limitations of realism altogether. In a production of

" Hamlet " he would not need to suggest the various parts of the palace at Elsinore ; he would simply convey an impression, in terms of form and colour, of what Hamlet means to him. This stagecraft, in the words of Kenneth Macgowan,[1] " sets itself to visualize the atmosphere of a play. Its artists aim to make, in the settings called for by the text, an emotional envelope appropriate to the dramatic mood of the author, a visualization in colour, line and light of the dominant emotions to be pictured by the actors."

It is here, perhaps, that the producer will achieve his greatest artistic satisfaction. For it is only in the theatrical convention of poetic drama that the grand conception of " Theatre," in which all the factors are truly interdependent and exploited to the full, may be completely achieved. But even here he will remember that the play itself must come first, and he must not in his enthusiasm be tempted to let the décor over-weight it.

[1] *The Theatre of To-morrow*, by Kenneth Macgowan. T. Fisher Unwin. 1923.

VII. FORM IN PRODUCTION

Up to this point we have dealt with the Content of a performance : we have explained how various aspects of the producer's work help the audience to appreciate the dramatic import of a play. Here we are concerned with a different kind of appreciation ; the appreciation of *how* things are said and done—the Form ; rather than of *what* is said and done—the Content.

The determination of the Form is influenced by the Content, obviously enough. But the pleasure to be derived from it is a pleasure entirely separate. We may listen to the sound of words beautifully spoken, and we may enjoy that sound without taking in the meaning of the words themselves : we may watch with pleasure the movements of an actor without having to realize the reason for those movements. Yet beautiful speaking will increase the value of the words spoken, and good movement will give an added significance to the action performed ; content and form, though separate, are interdependent.

To the actor Form appears under the guise of various accomplishments, taught under the names of Gesture, Movement, and Elocution. These cannot be explained within the scope of this book. The exact timing, for instance, of such a lovely line as King Lear's

> Thou'lt come no more
> Never, never, never, never, never !

cannot be expressed in words : it can only be done.

Such qualities can be taught—to those who have the instinct for them—by the appropriate instructors.

To the producer, however, Form appears in three aspects : (1) as a quality appearing in a performance in isolated patches, where it acts in a purely decorative capacity in the same way as a vivid piece of colouring in a picture ; (2) as the purely decorative quality in the *décor* and grouping, as distinct from their stimulative and interpretative capacities ; (3) as integral with the very structure of the performance, a quality analogous to the composition and design of a picture.

Isolated Examples of Form.

There may be moments in a performance when some particular effect will have a value of its own, apart from any value in expressing atmosphere, or plot, or character ; for example : a contrast of a high voice with one in low pitch, a movement of particular grace, a combination of movements, or a combination of voices. Such effects will often occur simply by chance ; and perhaps it is better so, for if they are used too consciously and too often they may obtrude too much upon the performance. In using them the wise producer does well to be sparing : there is an insolence in distracting an audience from attention to a play's substance.

Certain plays, however, do demand considerable insistence upon the manner. The highly stylized products of the dramatists of the seventeenth and eighteenth centuries are written in a convention for which a somewhat meticulous attention to the details of gesture and movement and elocution are particularly necessary. But with these the producer is not so much consciously imposing form, as interpreting the convention of a period to whose characters the elegant artificialities were second nature. Indeed, the convention of a play is really the only arbiter in determining the degree to which the audience should be conscious of the kind of form which we call style. The more theatrical and the less naturalistic a play may be, the more justified becomes an emphasis upon style and upon the formal effects of voice and of movement.

Form in Décor and Grouping.

This is not the place in which to deal with form in stage design, for it has been exhaustively explored elsewhere. It is enough to say that here, too, the producer must be careful. A sense of form in the creation of the grouping and setting is essential, in so far as it ensures that the pictorial aspect of a performance will compose into a stage picture that is pleasing to the eye : it becomes oppressive when it is too consciously expressed in such a way as to obtrude upon the spoken drama and to swamp it. The same will apply to the grouping of the characters. In most cases the stage picture which is most dramatic will also be the best from the point of view of composition. The producer's instinct will be his best adviser : if he has no instinct for form, no one will be able to teach it him.

Here again it is the convention of the play that must decide how much of the purely decorative element may be safely permitted in a setting. A play which is frankly artificial and mannered will reflect this quality in its appropriate *décor* : a play of " style " will demand a self-conscious air of style in its grouping.

Structural Form.

To the producer this is the most important aspect of form in the theatre. It is that quality which is so often loosely described as " rhythm," but which corresponds more nearly to design and composition in art.

Form in art—painting, for instance—consists in the relationship between various values of tone and colour and line : it will be influenced in any picture by the nature of that picture's representational intent, yet its significance as *design* will be a separate quality to be appreciated for itself alone. Form in the theatre also consists of the relationship between various values —theatrical values : and these values, too, are considered in their relationship apart from their purely dramatic and interpretative meaning.

The theatrical values are the " lines " and " tones " of performance. Varying shades of emotion, contrasts of any kind, a dramatic entrance or exit, a piece of grouping or a movement, the rise and fall of dialogue—each of these is a theatrical value which, considered apart from its dramatic significance, may be made to take its proper place in a performance almost as if it were a note in a sort of dramatic scale. Just as no single note in a tune has any meaning except in relation to the sequence of notes which follows it and precedes it, so has no theatrical value any *formal* significance unless it can be related to each of the other theatrical values in the performance. If this relationship exists, then to the pleasure of knowing that a given effect is inevitable because it is psychologically and dramatically right, is added the pleasure of knowing that it is also inevitable because it falls into its proper place in the creation of a pattern. And the perfection of the pattern lends its colour to the emotional content of the performance : in this way Content and Form are linked together.

The progression of a performance of a play should

move steadily and be varied but unbroken, in accord-
ance with some definite scheme. The nature of the
scheme is elastic, indeed, so elastic that it can scarcely
be expressed except in execution ; but whatever it
may be, there is one fixed law which it will have to
obey. This law is best expressed by a simile : *the
progress of any performance is like that of a road cross-
ing an island from one coast to another. The road may
go up hills and down again, but whatever its rise and fall
it must ultimately return to that level from which it
started—sea level. And for every ten feet of ascent there
must be, somewhere along it, a corresponding ten feet of
descent.*

In the progress of a performance " sea-level " corresponds to a level of apparent *normality* of speech
and movement and general behaviour of the characters,
to which they seem constantly impelled to return.
This is not necessarily the normality of real life, but a
level of performance at which, by comparison with
other levels, the tension is loosened and the characters
appear most at their ease. In all good plays this
quality is very evident : the scenes are written in such
a way that whatever flights they may make into the
dramatic, the emotional or the highly farcical, they
must return, if only for a space, to the ordinary,
after which the soaring process is repeated. This
rise and fall is necessary, not only because of the
necessity for contrast, not only because there is a
limit to the excitement of concentrated emotion
which an audience can stand and beyond which it
must demand relief ; but because the scheme of the
dramatist's own design demands it, for by varying
the degree and duration of his periods of excitement
and relief the author is building a pattern into the
structure of his play.

In most plays the level of *absolute normality* will be found only at the beginning and at the end, that is before the drama has properly begun, and after its knots have all been finally untied. In between, however, they will mostly be found to fall quite easily into scenes or "phrases," each of which rises to its own climax, and each of which is separated from the preceding and the following phrase by a subsidence to a level of *comparative normality* which is emphasized by the peaks of tension which bound it on either side. In this way the playwright creates his form by means of the varying relationships between certain *emotional values*.

Now the producer creates his form through the varying relationships between certain *theatrical values*, that is values not of emotion only, but of contrasts of speech and movement—and particularly the rise and fall and *tempo* of dialogue. Each of these theatrical values has its own normality : "normal" dialogue will be neither too fast nor too slow, neither too soft nor too loud, "normal" movement will be smooth, controlled and gentle. Here, too, the normality in many cases will be apparent through contrast rather than through any absolute quality. It will also vary according to the nature of the play. Normal dialogue will be quicker, for instance, in a play whose drama is upon the surface—such as a farce or a melodrama —than in one where the drama is submerged and the dialogue thoughtful.

The performance therefore—like the play itself— may be divided into phrases which are simply departures from this normality bounded by the inevitable return to it. Dialogue may start at a certain level of pace ; it may then increase and continue to increase until it reaches a climax of fast *tempo*, and then it may subside to its original level or somewhere near it. Similarly it may increase to a climax of great volume and then relapse to quietness. Movements in a scene may become quicker and quicker, or slower and slower, until at a climax they come to a turning-point and recede to normality. Grouping may assume aspects of great tensity, by concentrating the attention upon a particular person, or persons, or parts of the stage : then it may lose this quality and cease to possess any particular significance at all. Each of these " phrases " are in themselves emotional stimuli. Properly handled, they may create in an audience the same subtle quickening of the senses that we experience in listening to good music finely played.

Their nature and their degree, and their occurrence in any particular part of a performance will be largely influenced by the nature of the play : the comparatively broad scheme of emotional values created by the dramatist will act as a framework, upon which may be built the more detailed formation of theatrical values imposed by the producer. We have already shown that as a scene arrives at its emotional climax, so may its *tempo* increase or decrease, according to the nature of the scene. In the same way the emotional climax may be led up to by an increase or decrease of volume, and by each and all of the methods through which dramatic tension may be increased.

Thus the main framework in the formal structure of a performance consists of the phrases into which the dramatist has already divided his play before the producer has even touched it : as the main emotional values vary, so will the theatrical values vary with them. But within this framework exists a lesser, consisting of all the minor variations in significance and value of which dialogue is capable. Within each large phrase, itself based upon a phrase already created by the dramatist, may exist a number of smaller phrases which owe their being to such influences as the entrance of a new character, or the appearance of a new subject, or idea, or some change in the method of approach of one character to another, in short, any change of " angle," however slight. For example, in the excerpt from " Othello " quoted on page 26, the *main phrase* which the producer may emphasize begins at the beginning of the scene and continues up to the smothering of Desdemona. As we have seen, this main phrase is marked by a *general* increase in pace and volume. Within this main phrase there are four smaller phrases : the first, down to line 22, consists of the soliloquy, which is obviously a self-contained unit ; the second continues from line 23 to line 47 and consists of Othello's statement of his intention to kill Desdemona ; the third runs from this point until the end of line 75, and deals almost exclusively with Cassio and the handkerchief ; the fourth begins here and continues to the climax at the end. Even these phrases are capable of subdivision : the soliloquy falls neatly into two portions, divided by the kiss ; the lines beginning with Desdemona's " Talk you of killing ? " (see page 31) form a little phrase of their own ; so do those beginning with her " I never gave it him. Send for him hither ! " (page 32).

Each of these phrases has its own little climax to which it rises and from which it falls. For some, the boundaries of apparent and comparative normality are fairly well marked, viz. at the end of the soliloquy and at the end of the second phrase at line 47. For others the normality is comparative indeed, and scarcely apparent at all. Yet it does exist by implication : the last few lines of the third phrase deal with

Iago's supposed execution of Cassio, and, as we have seen (see page 33), they constitute a " breather," an interpolation, which is spoken *quietly* and *slowly* in a manner *apart* from the general vocal scheme of the scene. They therefore provide a comparative normality of voice and pace, by contrast with what has come before. With the fourth phrase and the little sub-phrases the return to apparent normality, though not obvious is also there : in this case it is accomplished through the dramatic pauses with which each phrase finishes. After the sweep of emotion to the climax of the smothering of Desdemona there is a pause of great length : this pause constitutes an apparent normality by contrast with the crescendo of pace and volume which precedes it.

The fact that the phrases in the structure of a performance may often be bounded by a dramatic pause brings us to the all-important question of *timing*. Up to now we have dealt with many uses of the pause, but we have never attempted, beyond the use of the words " long " or " short," to define what, in varying circumstances, governs its duration. For serving its purely dramatic function a certain latitude in the timing of a pause may be no hindrance. Provided it is long enough to do its work to provide clarity and put a proper interpretation on a line, it may not matter much if it is a trifle too long. But in its capacity as part of the framework upon which may be built some sort of form in a performance, the emphasis upon it is part of the pattern of the whole. This pattern must not be departed from : hence the duration of the pause is a definite matter, over which there can be no two opinions.

What governs this duration is the fact that every phrase in a performance must have a definite " outline." That outline, whatever its general nature may be, is in one particular governed by the nature of the audience itself. A phrase, be it broad or subtle, is an emotional, or a sensory, stimulus to the audience ; and an audience's feeling is easily roused, but not so easily subdued. It may easily be worked up to a state of excitement by a more or less gradual process, or it may be jolted into that state by some sudden dramatic occurrence ; but it will not quickly *subside* from that state ; it must be allowed to calm itself gently. Hence a phrase may rise gradually or steeply to its climax, but *in no case must its fall away from it be too sudden* —or bathos will result, since the audience will be continuing in a state of tension which the performance has already left behind, with a consequent complete loss of accord between audience and performers. Gradual subsidence from the climax of each phrase is therefore a necessity. That subsidence may be effected by the dialogue itself, as in the case of the first two phrases in the " Othello " scene, and the phrase from " Journey's End " quoted on page 73. Or it may be accomplished through the use of the dramatic pause, as in the last phrase of the " Othello " scene, or in the following :

STANHOPE. . . . D'you understand ? I'm fiddling with my revolver, d'you see ?—cleaning it—and it's going off by accident. It often happens out here. It's going off, and it's going to shoot you between the eyes.

HIBBERT (*in a whisper*). You daren't——

STANHOPE. You don't deserve to be shot by accident —but I'd save you the disgrace of the other way—I give you half a minute to decide. (*He holds up his wrist to look at his watch.*) Half a minute from now——

(*There is silence ; a few seconds go by. Suddenly* HIB-BERT *bursts into a high-pitched laugh.*)

HIBBERT. Go on, then, shoot ! You won't let me go
to hospital. I swear I'll never go into those trenches
again. Shoot !—and thank God——

STANHOPE (*with his eyes on his watch*). Fifteen more
seconds——

HIBBERT. Go on ! I'm ready——

STANHOPE. Ten. (*He looks at* HIBBERT, *who has closed
his eyes.*) Five.

(*Again* STANHOPE *looks up. After a moment he quietly
drops his revolver into its holster and steps towards
HIBBERT, who stands with lowered head and eyes tightly
screwed up, his arms stretched stiffly by his sides, his
hands tightly clutching the edges of his tunic. Gently
STANHOPE places his hands on HIBBERT'S shoulders.
HIBBERT starts violently and gives a little cry. He
opens his eyes and stares vacantly into STANHOPE'S
face. STANHOPE is smiling.*)

Good man, Hibbert. I liked the way you stuck that.

HIBBERT (*hoarsely*). Why didn't you shoot ?

STANHOPE. Stay here, old chap—and see it through . . .

The above is another quotation from " Journey's
End " : it comes from the first scene of the second act,
where Hibbert is trying to go sick in order to avoid the
coming attack. He has just attempted to get leave
from Stanhope, his superior officer ; Stanhope has
refused ; Hibbert has said he will defy him and has
actually attempted to leave the dug-out. And Stanhope is now telling him what will be the consequences
of desertion. This excerpt forms the end of a phrase.
Its climax is at that point where the audience is most
tense, wondering whether or not Stanhope is going to
shoot Hibbert—in short, during the pause on Stanhope's line : " Ten . . . five." The scene—quite a
long one—has worked up gradually to this climax from
a state of comparative normality some pages back.

Then, with one single line, the tension suddenly relaxes, Stanhope falls into his ordinary pleasant way of
speaking and says : " Good man, Hibbert. I liked the
way you stuck that." Such a sudden change is not
apparently a gradual subsidence at all, yet it is made
gradual by the dramatic pause which precedes it.
That pause will not only serve to point the suspense of
the climax, but, for every second that it continues
after it, it will help gently to slacken the suspense and
accomplish the gradual rounding off of the phrase.

The timing of the pause will depend therefore, not
only upon the period necessary to give the audience its
full measure of suspense, and to point the situation,
but upon the time needed to effect this gradual subsidence smoothly yet adequately. Such gauging is a
matter for great nicety of feeling : it demands some
sensitivity and the right instinct rather than calcula-
tion. Yet, to some extent, it can be calculated. A
phrase is like the coast-to-coast road, which has to
compensate for every foot of its ascent with an equiva-
lent foot, somewhere along its route, of descent. Its
fall from its climax is determined by the extent of its
rise to it. If the rise to the climax has been over a
long period, the fall will be greater, and the pause
consequently longer. Similarly the greater is the
climax itself the higher the peak to which it rises and
the greater is the fall : the longer, therefore, must be
the pause to " break " the fall. Another factor is
the degree of apparent normality to which it is
intended the phrase should subside. The greater the
normality, the greater the subsidence to it : if the
normality is merely comparative, the subsidence is
less, and therefore the length of the pause may be less.

The timing of the pause therefore assumes great
importance when it is realized that, not only is it

affected by what comes before it, but that it itself affects what comes after it. For example, in a series of phrases which go to make up one act of a performance, the degree of the climax in the first, and the length of time taken to reach it, will affect the length of the pause which follows it, and according to the length of this pause a greater or lesser degree of normality will be reached, which will affect the approach to the *next* climax in the *next* phrase, and so on. Thus a single error of timing is not confined to that part of the performance in which it occurs, but may affect a number of the phrases which come after it.

This interdependence does not only apply to the main phrases of a performance. Even the subtlest variations, though they may not have their bases in emotional counterparts created by the dramatist, yet depend for their effect upon the same principle. A phrase whose climax is a climax of pace and not of emotion—and whose quality is therefore purely formal —will need rounding off in the same way, either through a gradual decrease of pace or through a *pause* : a phrase whose climax is a subtle increase or decrease of volume will finish with a gradual lessening of volume, or else with a *pause*. All phrases, however small in degree, are able to stimulate an audience to some extent ; even if the stimulation is not conscious, its effect upon an audience is apparent in an added zest for the qualities of the performance. Therefore the rule will hold good—even when the pause becomes a mere taking in of breath—that the period of subsidence is longest where the climax is greatest, and vice versa. Sometimes, if the climax be great, more than one pause may be used to round off the phrase ; but again, as with the single pause, their duration will depend upon the degree of the climax and upon the degree of normality to which the phrase must return.

Just as there can be phrases of volume and of pace, so can there be " phrases " of movement and grouping. We know that very often a movement of one person towards another will tend to increase dramatic tension, while a movement away from a character and out towards the sides of the stage may tend to decrease it. When these movements are employed to effect a grouping emphasizing particular characters at moments of climax, such movements act in harmony with the phrases of volume and *tempo* and emphasize them. Sometimes, on the other hand, a good effect may be achieved by a sort of discord, in which *tempo* increases, but volume, unexpectedly, decreases ; while loose movements of characters away from each other actually emphasize the tension by an apparent denial of it. There is no limit to the variations which are possible, provided it is recognized that, generally speaking, all the theatrical values are interdependent : a slow scene will demand a faster scene to follow it, and the latter may be faster in proportion as the former may be slower : silence, when it ceases, will give an added value to speech ; the more lengthy the silence, the more vivid the speech ; the greater the degree of volume in one place, the greater the degree of quietness which should somewhere follow it.

In the complexity of the formal structure of a performance—in the interweaving of its three sets of values,[1] sometimes in harmony, sometimes in discord —lies the secret of the infinite variety which a truly vital piece of Theatre may be made to possess. This is not variety just for the sake of variety—though in a purely stimulative capacity this serves an essential

[1] i.e. *Tempo*, Volume, Movement.

purpose—but variety systematized into a design. Yet, paradoxically perhaps, the good producer is not too conscious in his work of the process which creates this design, although he should be sensitive to its results. For form must appear to be an integral part of a production, not an embellishment imposed upon it ; the producer who arbitrarily divides a play into sections and phrases is attempting to make rigid an art which is too essentially personal to be anything but fluid. There are no rules which have more exceptions than those of the theatre : the principles laid down in connection with form are particularly marked in this respect, and their purpose is almost entirely explanatory. It must be obvious that such things as *tempo*, tone, volume and movement are influenced by purely dramatic considerations as well as those related to design. Interpretation, simple stimulative dramatic contrast and clarity must all be weighed together in thinking out the treatment of the scene. The phrasing of a performance should suggest itself to the producer through the qualities of the play and the implications of those qualities.

Indeed, perhaps the only essential with regard to Form in production is that the producer should have a feeling for it. If he has this feeling, but is only dimly aware of it, then the principles that have been laid down may be of service to him, provided he is not too conscious of them during his actual work. But if his sensitivity is alive and kicking he will do well to forget them altogether, since the form which is appropriate to the play will suggest itself to him quite spontaneously. For Form in performance is as the shadow of the play itself ; it may vary in outline here and there, but in character it is definite and unique ; it belongs to one particular play and to no other. It is for the producer to perceive it, rather than to create it.

If, in perceiving it, he can express it, he will enhance enormously the value of his performance. An audience may not always be sufficiently attuned to appreciate the pattern of a performance, but they will always appreciate its beneficent results. A performance which is satisfying as a design will be all the more satisfying as an entertainment, or as an emotional and intellectual experience, even if that design is not recognized. For, only through a completeness of the design will appear that quality of the *inevitable, which is yet unexpected,* which is the quality of all supreme moments in the theatre. In those moments, the appreciation of what is done, and of the way it is done, fuses into one rich experience.

VIII. SOME SPECIAL PROBLEMS IN THE PRODUCTION OF COMEDY

THE word "Comedy" should not here be understood in that specialized meaning which the present fashion of theatrical nomenclature has given it : for the purposes of this chapter comedy may be said to embrace everything in the theatre which is capable of causing laughter, from "high comedy" to farce—in short, *the comic*.

Of all the conventions of the theatre, the comic convention is for the producer and actor the most difficult, and for that reason it has been left until late in this book to deal with some of the special problems which it presents. Comedy can only be successfully produced after a very thorough knowledge has been obtained of the general principles of ordinary theatre work ; and then success may depend, somewhat paradoxically, upon the degree to which those principles are forsaken. For comedy is a thing unique and apart from the rest of the theatre, and an audience's approach to it is fundamentally different from its approach to a "serious" play.

Henri Bergson said of the comic that "to produce the whole of its effect . . . it demands something like a momentary anæsthesia of the heart. Its appeal is to intelligence, pure and simple." These words explain the special position that comedy holds in the theatre, and the reason why it demands a special technique in its presentation. Comedy appeals to people, not through their emotions, but through their heads. This is not to suggest that the gentleman who amuses us by sitting on someone else's top hat demands of us a high degree of mental concentration, but merely to point out that in laughing at him we are not being emotional. If we were, we should immediately feel sorry at such wanton destruction ; but we are not sorry, because a " momentary anæsthesia of the heart " has seized us and made us incapable of feeling any emotion whatsoever.

The state of mind of an audience watching a comedy is an extremely critical state of mind. Unblurred by any emotion, always a possible obstruction to clear thinking, it is in a unique position to perceive the *manner* of a performance as well as its *matter* ; for that reason all the *formal* aspects of performance of comedy assume a very great importance, and such qualities as neatness of movement, economy of gesture, clarity of diction, an easy-flowing manner of speaking, smartness on the cues and all the other excellencies of technique need to be present in perfection. With an emotional play failures of this kind in the manner may often be compensated for by a great sincerity in the expression of the matter. Such distractions as false emphases, clumsy speaking or moving may be forgiven by an audience which is emotionally disposed to accept sincere acting : for, while an audience is engaged in some emotional reaction it is not in the least interested in technique, provided that technique is not sufficiently bad to hinder the emotional effect. Moreover, it may say, such clumsiness does after all happen in real life : how many people really speak well ; how many are able naturally to move gracefully ?

But comedy is the most artificial of the conventions. In it we are rarely asked to look upon life : we are asked to regard a world entirely separate from life which has its fascination precisely in that **Comedy an Artificial Convention** separation. The people of comedy neither act, speak nor behave as real people do. They make no mistakes of diction, they move always at the right moment and their every gesture and expression is always a perfect reflection of the situation in which they find themselves. If they have emotions, they are emotions from which we in the audience are removed. We regard them quite dispassionately : tears in comedy move us to laughter.

This lack of emotional intent behind the lines of comedy means that the time required for an audience to react to them is less ; for the minds of an audience are quicker than their emotions. Therefore the *general tempo* of comedy will be *quicker* than in other types of play, and each character will for the most part speak smartly on his cues. Pauses will, of course, occur, but their purpose will mostly be **Quick Tempo an Essential of Comedy** for the registering of comedy points, for obtaining and " feeding " laughs, and for planting material for laughs at later stages of the play. The general impression of the performance must never be one of slowness, for if an unnecessary pause occurs there can be nothing during its occurrence to which the audience may react. Deprived of its emotional content, which might give an audience something to ponder over during the gaps, comedy dialogue must have the continual stimulus of pace if it is to keep alive.

So much, then, for the general qualities of comedy— its artificiality and its denial of emotional appeal, resulting in performance in a necessity for perfection of style and a vigorous pace. Of its particular qualities, and of what constitutes the essentially comic much has been written, and much more might be written than could properly come within the scope of this book. For the purposes of the practical worker in the theatre,

Incongruity a Factor of Comedy however, it may be said that there is one factor which is nearly always common to every form of comedy, both of writing and of situation : this factor is an *incongruity* caused by some form of *contrast* which is *unexpected*, or *excessive*.

In the treatment of plays which are not comedy, incongruity is the very thing the producer strives to avoid. To this end he is careful to keep the play and its characters within the bounds of the convention which he and the author have decided is proper to them ; if he fails to do this he is likely to get laughter just where he does not want it. But with comedy both the producer and the author frequently do precisely the opposite. They begin a play in one convention, and then deliberately break it to create the incongruity which causes the comic. In farce it is the realistic convention which is rudely broken : the curtain usually goes up on an extremely detailed naturalistic setting in front of which appear people who seem for the moment to be in every respect normal, sane people. Then, suddenly, the convention is completely shattered ; everybody starts breaking china, dashing in and out of doors and getting unsuitably locked up with everybody else. It will be noticed that the realistic trappings of farce are nearly always particularly elaborate, heavy and convincing ; often indisputably real objects are brought on to the stage, such as aeroplanes and motor-cars. This is in order that the background may perpetuate in the mind of the audience the idea of realism, so that the contrast, between it and the fantastic happenings which take place before it, may be constantly emphasized. A farce played before a stylized background would lose a certain proportion of its comic value.

In farce the incongruity arises from the clash between a realistic and a fantastic convention : the conflict is in the plane of situation and action. As the humour becomes more subtle and approaches that of what we nowadays call " comedy " the conflict is lifted into the plane of dialogue and character. The present vogue for mediæval " costume " comedies written in modern colloquial English is an example of this. Audiences have got used to the convention that costume plays mean either Shakespeare or plays whose dialogue is in long literary periods and romantic clichés : consequently they laugh at the contrast between the twentieth-century naturalistic convention and the convention of " romantic drama." In the epigrammatic drawing-room comedy the conflict appears in another form : here the dialogue is usually too rich and too apt, too neat and too rounded ; it is deliberately in direct contrast to the more clumsy talk of real life.

The most frequent incongruities in modern comedy are to be found within the speeches themselves, and in the interplay of different conventions in the drawing of character. It is mostly with these that the producer is concerned.

Below is an example : [1]

MARIO. I begin to see, now, what I shall do.

SAVINA. You said you would kill me if I betrayed you :—your duty to " society." *Not* society : only vanity ;

[1] From " The Mask and the Face," by C. B. Fernald. Samuel French. Ltd.

not duty : only fear.   And your very fear of ridicule makes you ridiculous.

MARIO.   Do you think so ?

SAVINA.   And made me a little ashamed.

MARIO.   Did it ?   For the last time, then.   You are going away from here.

SAVINA.   Going away ?

MARIO.   Out of this house ; out of this country.

SAVINA.   Mario—— !

MARIO.   No one will know when or how or where you went.   Over the frontier in my car.   I shall drive it.   Then, I shall know how to do the rest.

SAVINA.   The rest ?   Maric, what do you mean ?

MARIO.   Nobody will laugh at me to-morrow.

SAVINA.   You make me afraid.

MARIO.   For your life ?   No.

SAVINA.   For you.   You are planning something absurd ; to save your face with the people who were here to-night.

MARIO (*cold*).   Be ready to leave this house in twenty minutes.

SAVINA.   But, Mario, you *can't* send me away like this !

MARIO.   Over the frontier you will take the train for Paris.   Go on till you reach London.   Never come nearer to me than that again.

SAVINA.   Mario, you can't.   This house is my home, my world, my everything.

MARIO.   You must cease to call yourself by my name.

SAVINA.   Mario, let me have until to-morrow.

MARIO.   The name you dishonoured.

SAVINA.   I did not dishonour it.   Why do you not honour my confession and my candour ?

MARIO.   I will see that you have money.

SAVINA.   But it's you I want.

MARIO.   Unless I hear that (*points off* R.) *he* has joined you (*with a shrug*), whoever he is.

SAVINA.   Mario, give me a few hours first.

MARIO.   I want you to be dead.

The above quotation is taken from the first act of the play. Its theme concerns a pompous Italian nobleman, Mario, who has always boasted that if ever his wife were to be unfaithful to him, he would kill her for her sin and take the consequences—penal servitude for life. When, however, an unfortunate circumstance leads him to suppose, quite wrongly, that she actually has deceived him, he lacks the courage of his convictions and dares not do what he considers his duty. But he is so frightened for his dignity that, rather than face his friends with an admission of cowardice, he has her removed abroad so that he may pretend to the world that he really has killed her.

This scene is an excellent test of a producer's mettle, since *it does not contain a single line which is in itself comic.* The whole phrase can easily be played as if it were perfectly serious, yet properly treated, it should provoke a continual chuckle from the audience.

One of the secrets of the comedy approach to the scene lies in deliberately contrasting the conventions in which the two protagonists play their parts. Savina is sincere and quite naturalistic : Mario is melodramatic and theatrical. The difference must be subtle in the extreme, or the scene becomes burlesque ; all that is wanted is for Mario to give just that little touch of exaggeration to his performance which will remove it the merest trifle from the naturalistic key in which Savina plays. When Mario is self-pitying he is a little more than reasonably so ; when he is dramatic he steps over the edge and becomes melodramatic ; when he commands it is as if he were Emperor of Rome, and so on. In this clash of conventions lies much of the comedy of these two characters.

There is comedy also in Mario's inhuman, almost grotesque, rigidity and setness of purpose ; in his mechanical churning out of words, oblivious to all her entreaties. This is a dressing up of one of the oldest causes of laughter—the low comedian's "gag," which turns any remark into the comic by simply continuing to repeat it over and over again at definite intervals.[1] Mario's rigidity should be reflected in the tone of his voice, which should hardly vary throughout the scene, except to become gradually more definite. Variety may be maintained, of course, by Savina, who, since she is playing naturally, will find no difficulty in making the proper dramatic contrasts.

Comedy will also arise from the incongruity between the *apparent* meaning upon the surface of a line and the *concealed* meaning beneath it :

MARIO. . . . and when a man makes himself ridiculous to his wife she very soon ceases to love him.

SAVINA. Oh, no, my dear Mario. Aren't you going to play ? You are so clever at poker.

In this instance the audience laughs, mainly because it is sharing a secret with one of the characters of the play—a thing which it loves to do.

The words " Oh, no, my dear Mario," ostensibly convey Savina's *general* disagreement with Mario's general statement. But actually they convey her own particular reaction at that particular moment, which is : " Yes, darling, you think that ; but really and truly you are making yourself rather ridiculous now, yet in spite of that I can manage to love you." With her mouth Savina gives to the words their *general* significance : with her eyes and the tone of voice she uses she indicates, quite clearly, their *true* meaning. In doing this

[1] Bergson lays down this "mechanical inelasticity" as being a fundamental quality of the comic.

she is taking the audience into her confidence, and they laugh with her at Mario's expense.

Here is another example from the same play :

MARIO.   I want you, Franco, because——
FRANCO.   Because what ?

(MARIO *looks at him calculatingly.*)

MARIO (*after a moment*).   Because I have killed my wife.
FRANCO.   Killed your—— What are you saying ?
MARIO.   My wife : she betrayed me. I killed her.
FRANCO.   It isn't true. You're mad !
MARIO.   Killed her—here in this room.
FRANCO.   When ? How ? Mario—— ?

(MARIO *watches the effect as he makes up his story.*)

MARIO.   She was in her room—with a man. I surprised them. The others kept me from killing her then.
FRANCO.   A man—— ?
MARIO.   Then, when I was alone with her, I seized her by the throat. I can feel my nails now, cutting into her flesh. I dragged her out against the balustrade. I pushed her back and strangled her—till she was dead and limp in my arms. Then I——
FRANCO.   Good God ! Good God ! Where is she now ?
MARIO.   Eh ? (*Looking round.*) I don't know.
FRANCO.   Don't *know* !
MARIO (*pointing vaguely over the lake*). I don't know where. Somewhere—far out : at the bottom of the lake.
FRANCO.   No one saw you ?
MARIO.   No : too dark. That is all. (*He folds his arms.*)

A number of different factors contribute to the comedy of this scene. To begin with, Franco is the man who, unknown to Mario, attempted unsuccessfully to be Savina's lover. Initially, therefore, there is a grotesque contrast in the double deception of the two

men : the audience share a secret with Mario, for they
know that Savina has not been murdered ; they also
share one with Franco, for Mario does not know that
Franco is, at any rate in intention, the guilty man.
There is also the conflict in the conventions in which
the two men are acting. Franco is sincere and really
frightened : Mario is playing a part, and is rather
enjoying himself ; moreover, he is maintaining his own
character of exaggerated pompous grandiloquence, as
against Franco's more simple naturalism. Then there
can be comedy in the phrasing and timing of the scene.
As it progresses Mario builds up his horrible tale, piling
detail upon detail picturesquely and melodramatically :
with his long speech the climax approaches ; he becomes louder and more definite as he seems to lead into
his climax with the lines

I dragged her out against the balustrade. I pushed her
    back and——

and at this point, *for a second only*, he hesitates ; what
did he do to her, he wonders. Then quickly his
imagination carries him on :

    and *strangled* her——

But in that momentary ceasing of the natural flow of
the phrase comedy has stepped in and made the whole
speech ridiculous. The formal structure of the phrase
has been abruptly and unexpectedly broken by a shattering of the normal timing of melodrama. But bravely
Mario carries on—already the audience should have
begun to laugh ; he reasserts himself, regains the flow
of his language and is proceeding towards the building
up of a second climax when Franco interrupts with an
exceedingly awkward question :

    Where is she now ?

Mario had not thought of that, and his imagination is not equal to the task of thinking of it now. He answers stupidly and prosaically :

I don't know.

Once again the climax is ruined, and the normal sweep of the phrase stopped : but here the shattering is more complete, for not only has the timing been broken unexpectedly, but the convention has been broken unexpectedly too ; from the grandiloquent key Mario has been suddenly forced into the merely conversational. He continues in this vein, vaguely groping for a solution. Suddenly he thinks of the one statement that for the moment nobody can disprove :

Somewhere—far out : at the bottom of the lake.

The audience should almost hear his sigh of relief. He has come out of a tight corner, but he is safe once more, and with his final lines he regains his old composure and his old pomposity, and stands there complacent and ridiculous, his arms folded like Napoleon.

Comedy may come, therefore, not only from an incongruity between conflicting conventions, but from the contrast between the expected timing of a phrase and its actual timing. Consequently it is sometimes possible to achieve the comic by defying those principles of form and clarity which have already been explained : the expected pause after the climax of a scene or of a line, and those pauses which in naturalistic dialogue would separate two differing ideas—these may be ignored to obtain a comic effect. Earlier in the same act of this play there is a scene that shows this. It is Mario's first entrance : his guests are talking about a pair of Americans who are indulging in an illicit honeymoon in the neighbourhood :

WANDA. They say that woman's husband was a dreadful man.

MARIO. Man? Why do you call him a man? No, Wanda. That pair have been about the lake for three weeks. If her husband had been a man he would have followed her to Como by now.

GEORGES. Followed her?

MARIO. And he would have killed her.

PIER (*speaking of* MARIO'S *attitude of mind*). Eleventh century A.D.

FRANCO. You have said that sort of thing before, Mario; do you mean it?

MARIO. I do not speak lightly on such matters.

If this excerpt were not regarded as comedy the procedure in the phrasing of it for production would be as follows: the lines " and he would have killed her " are the most dramatic in the scene, and are led up to by the first three speeches. They would consequently form the climax of a phrase: being dramatic, and important, they would be followed by a pause, which would also serve to mark the period of subsidence from the climax, as well as to separate the idea of Mario's sentiments from the conflicting idea of Pier's sentiments.

Since it is comedy, however, the method is entirely different. Mario is not allowed the dignity and emphasis of a pause after his six dramatic words. Pier steps in with his lines at once, thus destroying the expected timing and deliberately causing the two conflicting ideas to cut across each other. The phrase ends, therefore, not after the " dramatic " line from Mario, but after the " funny " line from Pier: and unless that line *does* come extremely quickly on Mario's cue, the laugh will inevitably be lost.

Here is another example in Lady **Kitty's speech**

from Act One of Somerset Maugham's " The Circle " :

LADY KITTY.   I'm never nervous.   I'm a born actress. Of course, if I had my time over again I'd go on the stage. You know, it's extraordinary how they keep young. Actresses, I mean.   I think it's because they're always playing different parts.   Hughie, do you think Arnold takes after me or after his father ?   Of course I think he's the very image of me.   Arnold, I think I ought to tell you that I was received into the Catholic Church last winter.   I'd been thinking about it for years, and last time we were at Monte Carlo I met such a nice Monsignore. I told him what my difficulties were and he was too wonderful.   I knew Hughie wouldn't approve so I kept it a secret.   (*To* ELIZABETH.)   Are you interested in religion ? I think it's too wonderful.   We must have a long talk about it one of these days.   (*Pointing to her frock.*)   Callot ?

Compare this long speech with that from " Uncle Vanya " on page 19.   In this there are no less than five completely separate ideas, yet to separate any one of them would be fatal to a successful comedy effect, which consists solely in a ridiculous juxtaposition of themes which really have nothing to do with each other.   The entire speech should therefore be rattled off rapidly and with little regard for the principles of clarity and contrast.

The essentially artificial nature of much comedy must never be forgotten ;   for instance :

TEDDIE.   Oh, but I love it out there.   England's ripping to come back to, but I couldn't live here now.   It's like a woman you're desperately in love with as long as you don't see her, but when you're with her she maddens you so that you can't bear her.

If, through inexperience or bad craftsmanship, a playwright were to allow such a speech to appear in a naturalistic play, the producer would cause it to be played slowly and gropingly. The speaker would have to cloak the facile quality of his similes by appearing to feel for them in his mind. But the speech is from " The Circle," and Somerset Maugham has written his entire play in an artificial convention : hence there is every reason for speaking it flowingly and well with every regard for its tone and cadence. Such is the producer's method with all " smart " and epigrammatic comedies, the plays of Oscar Wilde, the Restoration Comedies and the like.

So much for some of the factors which cause laughter. There remain two very practical aspects of comedy production : the actual method of " getting laughs " and the " feeding " or husbanding of the laughter when it comes.

Some lines will create laughter no matter how badly they are delivered : others will have no effect at all unless they are properly " pointed." And the subtler the wit of the line, the more carefully must

Getting Laughs it be pointed. Comedy points are just like any other important effect upon the stage ; they require emphasis in precisely the same way ; and the principles behind their emphasis are simply those of clarity and suspense.[1] That is, there must be a dramatic pause (actually, of course, it is no more than a breath) *before* the line which is intended to get the laugh, followed by another and longer pause *after* the line, during which the line may have its full effect upon the audience. The effect is, of course, laughter : and the pause must last exactly long enough to let the laughter have its way. *The scene should not continue until the laughter begins appreciably to die down*, otherwise the next lines will be lost in the noise of the

[1] See pages 16–18.

audience. On the other hand, the pause for the laugh must not be longer than is absolutely necessary, or the pace of the performance will suffer. This waiting for the laughs seems to present difficulties for some actors, who persist in treating it as if it were a very special and arduous technique of comedy acting. If it could only be regarded as a perfectly normal and logical application of the principle of clarity such misapprehension might easily be dismissed. For it is really very simple, and can be summed up in the maxim of the old touring troupers : " Tell 'em (the audience) you're going to do it : then do it : then tell 'em you've done it." If producer and actor apply this—with a reasonable subtlety of course—they cannot make a mistake.

An example of how to obtain a difficult laugh occurs in Quintero's " The Lady from Alfaqueque " :

NICOLÁS. Yes . . . and now cry ! It only wanted that ! I'd better go out and take a walk.

BLANCA. Do !

NICOLÁS. It'll give you a chance to cheer up.

BLANCA. And it'll give you a chance to cool down. Good-bye.

FERNANDITA. Now, now . . . don't part like this. What a storm in a teacup ! You want to have children and he doesn't. Very well, then, you must compromise. That's what married life is . . . compromise.

A girl and her bad-tempered fiancé are quarrelling about the question of children, and the girl's guardian, Fernandita, is making a well-meaning attempt to pour oil on the waters. There is no obvious laugh here. But a laugh can be obtained upon the line : " Very well, then, you must compromise," for there is a definite absurdity in compromising over whether or not children shall be born. If ever a word were unsuitable and incongruous the word " compromise " is so here. Yet the joke takes a little time to become apparent to an audience, and consequently it is essential to point it. This is done by simply saying :

You must . . . compromise.

If during the little pause the actress is seen to be groping, a trifle painfully, for the word which is most apt for the occasion, she is certain to obtain a laugh when she falls upon the one word of all words which is ridiculously wrong.

Difficulties sometimes arise with lines which are capable of producing two or three laughs all fairly close to each other ; for an audience's capacity for laughter is oddly limited. There appears to be a definite degree to which they are capable of laughter : if there are three jokes to one speech they will divide their laughter between them, but the laughs will be small in volume and duration. If, however, there is but one joke— and that where it should be, as a climax, at the end of the speech—the laugh will be long and loud.

For example, these lines from " The Merry Wives of Windsor " :

MISTRESS QUICKLY.   Marry, sir, I come to your worship from Mistress Ford.

FALSTAFF.   Mistress Ford !   I have had ford enough ; I was thrown into the ford ; I have my belly full of ford.

Falstaff, it will be remembered, speaks these heart-felt lines after his unfortunate contact, within the buckbasket, with the River Thames.   Unless they are correctly timed, the audience will tend to begin laughing upon the words " I have had ford enough," and to laugh even more on " I was thrown into the ford," with the result that the last line, which is intrinsically the most comical of all, will be lost in their own hilarity.

The producer may tackle this problem in three ways. He may decide that the last line is the best of the three, and, sacrificing the other two, may concentrate all his effect upon it, to get one big laugh. In this case he will ask his Falstaff to run quickly through the speech to a climax on the last line, to speak that last line upon a top note, and to pause after it while the laugh takes place. Or he may decide that the second line—" I was thrown into the ford "—has some value, and that consequently it is worth while to try for two laughs of a lesser degree. In this case he will treat this line as the climax of the speech, cause his actor to take it on his top note, *wait for the laugh*, and then to add, *as an afterthought* and with the contrast of a lower, more confidential tone, the last line. The contrast of tone in the last line will serve to emphasize it, so that, quite possibly, the laugh here may be as big as with the first method. This way is probably the best. But a third would be possible : to try for three small laughs—one on each line—and to wait for the laugh after each. This method is the most difficult, for the second and third lines would probably have to be forced over—" plugged " is the theatrical expression—in order to cap the noise of the laughter preceding them. This might easily result in exaggeration and over-playing.

Of comedy it may be said, as of so many of the qualities demanded of the producer, that an instinct for it is worth all the theatrical tricks put together, and that a " sense of comedy " both in producer and actor is more than necessary. Such is obvious. But instinct is not enough : it cannot be too firmly stressed that before a producer may give free expression to his sense of comedy, he must be sure enough of his technique to ensure *mechanical perfection* in his performance. Therefore let him remember the importance of pace, of firm unhesitant speaking, of neat movements, of tidy entrances and exits, of repose (except where movement conveys something or cannot be noticed), and, above all, *of waiting for the laughs.*

IX. PRODUCTION PRACTICE

In practice the work of the producer divides itself into two periods : a difficult period of intensive work upon the manuscript of the play to be produced, and an easier period of actual rehearsal, during which demands are made rather upon his dramatic instinct than upon his thought.

The Manuscript.

Before the first rehearsal the producer is expected to have all the mechanical factors in the production plotted and fairly definite. Subsequently he may, and probably will, alter details ; but unless he can give his actors the impression that he is able to solve all the problems which will confront them in the first rehearsals—such as movements, entrances and exits, etc.—he will lose their confidence at the very beginning.

He reads the play for the first time ; he reads it, just as he would a novel, for his own pleasure, without effort. As he reads, vague images of the appropriate setting and of the positions of the characters at certain dramatic moments will probably begin to form themselves in his mind. The characters themselves will suggest their own personalities to him, and, as his first impressions of the play will be his nearest approach to the reaction which it will later have upon the audience, he proceeds to cast those characters in his mind with the actors which seem to him most suitable. As he examines the stage directions of the author he makes a mental note of whether or not they will prove practical in the theatre. In many cases he decides that their value is purely decorative, and proceeds to forget them.

He now definitely decides upon his cast, and having stoically surrendered to the necessary compromises in this matter, he reads the play a second time. He has already progressed one stage in his transformation of the manuscript into *a piece of Theatre*, for instead of thinking in terms of the author's characters, he is thinking in terms of parts as portrayed by particular actors. As he reads, he thinks of the personalities of the various performers and begins to correlate them with the characters they are supposed to represent. The pictorial side of the production forms more clearly in his mind, and at certain points in the script he may mark a few positions and moves where they seem to be wanted. The formal structure, too, shows itself a little ; he may note tentatively a few pieces of phrasing, a crescendo or two, or an increase or decrease of pace.

He is now ready to begin the real work. Up to this point he has scarcely had to labour ; he has merely gratefully accepted the kind promptings of his dramatic instinct, which he must now start to put into practice. He proceeds to design his setting. He now knows his play fairly well : he is acquainted with its convention, its atmosphere, its *locale*, the number of entrances required and the number of characters who are going to act before it. Taking all these factors into consideration, together with a regard for contrast and a pleasurable form and colour, he draws a ground plan, and possibly an elevation ; then he makes and paints a model to scale. In his colouring he is careful to consider the nature and quality of the lighting he will use. (The scheme of lighting he will, of course, have evolved as part of the designing of the set.)

His task is now to work out in detail each movement, and the complete phrasing and timing of the play, with all the necessary contrasts of voice, of movement, and of grouping. If his dramatic instinct is sound, most of the *tempo* and contrasts will suggest themselves to him ; his real struggle comes with the evolving of the movements. For he must remember that every movement in the production must seem natural ; yet, for the purposes of contrast and interpretation and of form he will wish to manœuvre his characters into arbitrary positions : therefore he must succeed in reconciling the two sets of influences behind each step that they take.

It is here that his model becomes extremely useful to him ; for his best method is to sit down with his manuscript, his model before him, complete with all the necessary furniture or other features of the scene, and to imagine as he reads that a miniature performance is taking place before his eyes. He will let his characters move in his mind's eye precisely as they would naturally seem inclined to move. Remembering the general principles behind movement, its capacity as a factor in interpretation, and the necessity for the avoidance of distraction, he will for a time plot down movements—tentatively—which the dialogue naturally suggests to him. For a time he will continue quite comfortably, until suddenly he finds that his characters have tied themselves up into knots, that they have become bunched up in corners, or that someone about to make an effective exit cannot do so because he is barricaded behind a chair and a table. Undaunted, the producer then retraces the steps of his imaginary performance until he comes to that point in the scheme of movement where the trouble began, and here he stops for a moment and thinks. Up to this point the movements are quite sound, for they are spontaneous and prompted by the dialogue ; but an alternative must be found for the move which started the complications, or else an alternative spot in the dialogue from which a move may be made. After some thought he will discover perhaps that an unconscious movement in one direction will serve him just as well as a conscious movement in another served him before ; or possibly he will be able to keep one character quite still and to move another instead ; keeping the principles behind movement always in mind, he will be able to find a way out of the difficulty. He may now let his characters move on once more of their own accord. His next problem may be that for a certain situation he wishes a particular grouping, and that his characters have somehow tiresomely chosen to sort themselves out in a manner completely contrary to his wishes. Once again he retraces his steps, finds the source of the difficulty, chooses his alternative moves, and fits them into his scheme. And in this way he works through the play.

At first sight this method may seem long and even wasteful. Instead of allowing the characters such licence, why, it may be asked, should not each movement be worked out with an eye to its later consequences and the entire range systematically constructed so as to avoid doing so much work twice ? The answer is that such complete systematizing would inevitably result in an appearance of artifice : the characters would seem to move far too mechanically, and behind each step taken by the actors the producer's will would be embarrassingly apparent. On the other hand, the method outlined above will ensure the greatest degree of ease and spontaneity in the movements. Moreover, with some practice, the producer will find that the knots into which he gets his characters become fewer and fewer ; he will soon acquire an instinct for recognizing the right move and distrusting the wrong one. So much is simply a matter for common sense : if a character has to make an exit within half a page, a move which takes him far away from a door and behind some furniture is obviously wrong. Soon the producer will find that most of the moves he decides upon need not be tentative at all, and he will plot them confidently in his script in the knowledge that they are right because they are natural and yet fulfil their purpose.

When he has completed this process his manuscript will be fully marked with symbols, such as " ⌢ " (a pause), " Xs R." (crosses to stage right, that is the right-hand part of the stage from the point of view of the actor), " D.L." (down-stage left), " R.C." (right centre of stage), " ⌒ " (Crescendo), " acc." (speed up *tempo*) and other abbreviations of his own invention. He will use abbreviations or numbers for his furniture, so that the position of every character at every moment of the play is recorded concisely and clearly. Nothing he has done will be irrevocable, but he will probably not have to depart far in rehearsal from his present plan. And now, nothing can crop up in rehearsals which can puzzle him or present any problem with which he cannot deal promptly and on the spot.

After a further reading, in which he fixes the psychology of the characters firmly in his mind and makes sure that the character of the play is reconciled to the work he has already done, he is prepared for the first rehearsal.

Rehearsals.

With his actors sitting around a table he now holds a reading of the play. They have probably had their parts for some days, and each actor will have formed his own idea of the character he is playing. The producer notes each rendering to see how it corresponds with his own conception. The individualities of the actors and their attitudes towards the play and towards their parts bring him new impetus. Little qualities of voice and *tempo* suggest themselves to him, prompted by the actors' readings : he stores them in his mind, ready to bring them out at the appropriate moment. Where an actor is uncertain about a particular character he explains his own view to him, and in subsequent discussion round the table the general attitudes of all towards their parts are finally settled.

The next day the first true rehearsal takes place. The producer devotes this entirely to putting into practice the scheme of movement he has already evolved : ignoring everything except the moves, he lets the actors sort themselves out. Here and there he makes an emendation. Perhaps he notices that some entrance is not so effective as he thought it might be : remembering that an entrance and the subsequent five minutes do more than the whole of the rest of the part to establish a character's personality, he makes the alteration that is necessary. Sometimes an actor finds himself uncomfortable in doing some manœuvre : if this is so, then the movement is probably wrong, for actors usually possess an instinct in these matters ; so the change is made and compensated for somewhere else. The producer may find that a piece of grouping which seemed to him attractive in the small scale of the model is not proving so in the large scale of the rehearsal room or stage. He alters a character here and there and puts it right. Meanwhile the stage manager is plotting down the movements in the prompt copy and the actors plot theirs in their parts. If the producer has worked out his scheme properly in advance the alterations will be few, and the production is soon "roughed out," ready for serious work.

When the movements are determined and proved to be sound, the producer begins to bring to the surface the formal and interpretative scheme in his mind. From now onwards he must bear in mind the proper relationship between producer and actor. He will find that a workable principle in the practice of production is *to see that the actor agrees with him about any particular effect that is desired, but to leave to the actor's own judgment the method of obtaining that effect.* The actor knows his own material best and should be allowed to use it in his own way without the producer's interference; but, on the other hand, if he cannot be made amicably to agree with and to understand the fundamental bases of the play and of his part, and to perceive the proper relation of his part to the whole, then that actor should be replaced by another who can.

The limitations of the actor's own personality will undoubtedly modify the scheme of the producer, who in many cases will have to be content with compromise. But the more suitably cast an actor may be, the more likely is he to bring his own effects into line with those the producer has thought out. In any case compromise is better than the result of trying to force an actor to do something which feels unnatural to him. The producer must realize that actors, like the play itself and the stage upon which it will be performed, are his material, and that every material has its limitations; his art consists largely in making those limitations serve his purpose in spite of themselves.

In these early stages of rehearsal he will take care not to tell his actors too much at a time. Although the entire performance is already beginning to live in his mind, he must remember that actors can only take production in comparatively small doses. The actor, unlike the producer, is regarding the play subjectively from his own angle, and at this stage is occupied with many other matters beyond the interpretation of his part. He is thinking of his moves and his positions, of the stage properties that he will use later on, and of where and how he will use them : he is reading his lines from a part which he has to carry awkwardly about with him, and is at the same time trying to get some idea of those lines into his head. So the producer does not harry and fuss him with too much detail of characterization, but leads him, gradually, towards complete realization. Beyond a certain point he will often allow mistakes to pass by, in order to correct them upon another occasion when the actor is perhaps fresher and more receptive. With experience he attains an insight into the mentality of the actor, which will show him just how much he can tell him on any single day, and just that point at which to tell him any more would be a mere waste of time.

The producer will watch his actors very carefully to see what effects they may instinctively bring to their performances, for at the beginning of rehearsals, the *natural* effects of any actor may be of the utmost value to him ; being usually spontaneous they will very often be right and worthy of incorporation into the general scheme. In the later stages the actor will have thought out his effects instead of feeling them : he may have thought them out painstakingly but wrong, and the producer will kindly but firmly have to put them right.

When the period of rehearsals is about half over, all

that the producer has had in his mind should have been communicated to his cast, and the actors should possess a general idea of what they are supposed to be doing. For a spell rehearsal hours are shortened to allow as much time as possible for " study "—the learning of the lines. The actors begin to come without their books and to stumble through their parts. For some days the producer relaxes his insistence, and leaves them alone to become easy with their words.

Then the form of the rehearsals changes. Mistakes are no longer passed over. Whereas before, the play was taken on each occasion in its entirety, so that a sense of cause and effect and of its general structure could be maintained by both producer and actors, now it is rehearsed in acts and scenes and even in phrases. What begin to matter now are the *tempo* and the contrasts of dialogue. The producer starts to build up the emotional scenes, and to see that in the playing of them the actors have plenty of force in reserve so that the proper climaxes can be emphasized. He begins to put on pace : for before there can be any contrast of pace the pace must be present, and up to now the performers have not had sufficient command of their words to begin to think of it. This period is exceedingly trying for all concerned. Scenes are performed over and over again : a single " dry " is the signal for a return to the beginning of the scene or even to the beginning of the act. Finally a state is reached where each actor is word perfect, or nearly so, and able if necessary to speak so quickly on his cue that he is almost cutting in on the man who spoke before him. Now the producer begins to smooth out and model the performances ; to quicken somebody here and slow up somebody there, to obtain his crescendos and time his pauses.

Throughout he keeps continual watch upon the characterizations of his cast, lest any part of the play should slip from its proper convention, or any character become inconsistent with his intentions and those of the author. At this point he will probably have to bear with a constant flow of suggestions from the actors, who are just beginning to become sufficiently acquainted with their own parts to start attempting to improve those of other people—as well as their own. He will not turn a deaf ear, but will consider them carefully. Sometimes he will receive an idea of some value ; more often he will have to reject the suggestion as the effort of some actor to make the part " fatter " than it was intended to be. Of greater value to him will sometimes be the suggestions which are hinted at rather than consciously expressed : a half-felt, tentative movement or gesture from an actor he may often take, turn over in his mind, and return to him as a finished effect, or piece of business.

At this point the producer must change his angle of vision. Up to now he has regarded the production from the viewpoint of one of the workers in it : he must now adjust his attitude to the performance, stand outside it, and regard it as if he were an enlightened member of the audience.

He ceases to direct rehearsals from the stage, sits at the back of the auditorium, and from now on *takes care not to interrupt the actors, whatever they do, until the end of a scene or other natural break in the play*. For by now the actors are beginning so to identify themselves with their parts and with the flow of the action, that any interruption of the flow upsets their playing and their feeling for the scene : later the producer will interrupt at the ends of the acts only, and will make notes of the points with which he wishes to deal.

This is the crucial period of rehearsals. From his new position at the back of the auditorium the producer will notice many things that before escaped him. Many days of hard work may have caused the actors to think more in terms of technique than in terms of results ; from his new vantage point the producer can supply a corrective. He may find a tendency to be too glib ; previous insistence upon pace and assurance may have created mechanical efficiency at the expense of conviction and spontaneity. Since he is now sure of his pace he may remove the effect of glibness by slackening it a little here and there. It is now that a further adjustment of the *tempo* and the variations of volume may take place. Contrasts and pauses which seemed suitable at close quarters may not make themselves sufficiently felt at the back of the theatre : these are corrected and the performers tested for variety and audibility. A final balance must be struck between all the factors which go to the make-up of a performance : form must not be too insistent at the expense of the interpretation : the grouping must maintain a pleasant aspect without showing the obviousness of artifice ; above all, the characterization and the intentions of the author of the play must still keep their integrity.

At last comes the dress rehearsal. The scene is set ; the lighting, which was evolved when the setting was designed, has been rehearsed and adjusted. The curtain is ready to rise. If possible, a small audience of privileged persons is present, so that the producer may test its reactions to the performance. For, after all, the audience is one of the most important factors in the theatre. The actors may play their parts excellently, but unless the audience plays its own part just as well the performance is certain to be a failure. The performance depends so much upon the audience : the audience depends so much upon the performance. And nobody, not the author, nor the producer, nor the actors, can be quite certain of what the audience's reaction will be. The producer, as a specialist, has made it his business to anticipate this unknown quantity, and the measure of his success lies in the degree of his correct anticipation. At the dress rehearsal he will probably find that in the main the audience has corroborated him by reacting where he hoped it would ; but he cannot always tell the *degree* to which it will react ; hence, after the rehearsal is over, slight changes of emphasis and *tempo*—particularly in connection with the timing of the dramatic pauses—may be found necessary. If the play is a comedy the audience can be all the more helpful, for the laughs can be definitely located—or rather some of the laughs, for a small audience will not laugh so often as a large one—and these can be marked in the script to give the actors some indication of what they may expect at the public performances.

When the dress rehearsal is over, and the final details have been at last adjusted, the producer must leave the rest to fate. If he is wise he will bother the actors no more, for theirs is the burden now. A last-minute change will be fatal, for it will only worry the performers and cause them probably to make bigger blunders in other directions. And worse, it will lay the producer open to the charge of not knowing his own mind.

The producer who seems uncertain of his own intentions will always lose the confidence of his actors ; and that confidence is his most valuable asset. It is for this reason that a thoroughness in the preliminary work upon the manuscript is of such very great importance. With the faith of his company, the good producer can obtain from them just exactly what he wants. There is no need for him to behave like a drill-sergeant ; he should never be so conscious of his own dignity that he cannot condescend to intelligent argument over points of difference. An actor may often disagree with a producer over points in his performance, and the producer should take an especial care in sorting out the trouble in friendly and sympathetic discussion. The occasions upon which an actor should be forced to do something which he does not wish to do are extremely rare. In many cases the actor may be right, and the producer should not be afraid to admit it. In many others a lucid explanation of *why* the producer may wish him to do a certain thing will result in his agreement. Intelligent actors quite naturally do not like to do things which seem to have no reason, and it is a fault of the martinet producer that he treats his actors like machines and forces them into actions of which he gives no explanation.

The best producer is undoubtedly he who produces without fuss, who controls without commanding, and who draws results from his players without always letting them realize just how much he is affecting their performance. For not his least important asset is an understanding of human nature. Actors, it may be said without offence, whether they are amateurs or professionals, are not entirely devoid of vanity : they will nearly always be happier if they think that they themselves have achieved something which the producer has really achieved for them. If he is a wise man he will allow them to continue in their illusion ; for, after all, if he wishes to obtain credit and recognition for everything that he does, he should really have chosen another occupation.

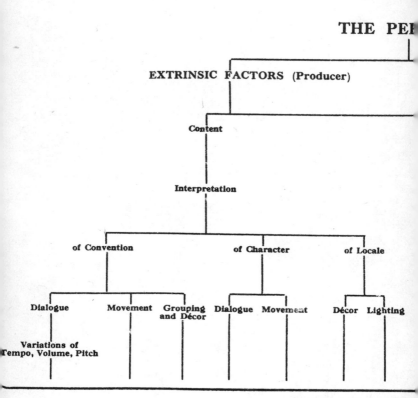

EXTRINSIC FACTORS (Producer)

Content

Interpretation

of Convention — of Character — of Locale

Dialogue — Movement — Grouping and Décor — Dialogue — Movement — Décor — Lighting

Variations of Tempo, Volume, Pitch

"DRAMATIC

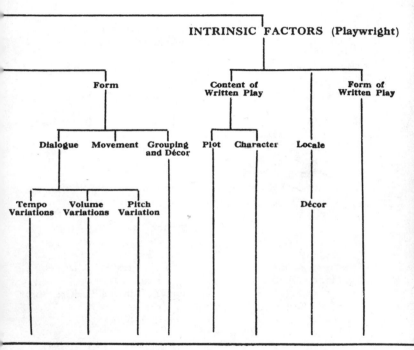

INTRINSIC FACTORS (Playwright)

Form

Content of Written Play

Form of Written Play

Dialogue Movement Grouping and Décor

Plot Character

Locale

Tempo Variations Volume Variations Pitch Variation

Décor

CONTRAST"

INDEX